ARCHITECTURE MANAGEMENT BODY OF KNOWLEDGE

AMBOK™ Guide
for Information Technology

ARCHITECTURE MANAGEMENT INSTITUTE

by Issam Thabit

Architecture Management Body of Knowledge:
AMBOK™ Guide for Information Technology

© 2011 Architecture Management Institute

ISBN: 978-0-9868626-0-1

Published by:

Architecture Management Institute
999 Collip Circle, Suite 101, Box 35
London, Ontario, N6G 0J3, Canada

E-mail: info@it-ami.org
www.it-ami.org

Printed in the United States of America

DEDICATION

This book is dedicated to the discipline of IT architecture and to the associated IT architects who chose this profession in order to make a difference. This difference will determine how information technology systems and components are architected, using strong foundational knowledge and processes. We hope that by planting the first seed with the AMI book of knowledge we will aid in establishing a strong foundation for the IT architecture discipline.

To have strong roots, we require fertile lands, ample water, and a strong sun. This is the formula needed to create an environment capable of erecting a well established tree that can withstand the challenges of time and nature. Architecture Management Institute's vision, support, and commitment will provide the strong sun necessary to clear the path and shed the light on the future of IT architecture. Organizations, individuals, and groups both locally and globally will provide the fertile lands by sharing their knowledge, experiences, and expertise. Everyone's commitment and continuous support will provide the ample water required for this formula to succeed. Let us begin the journey of establishing a global standard for IT architecture and uniting the architects' voices.

NOTICE: AMI and AMBOK™ GUIDE

Architecture Management Institute encourages readers to send comments, feedback and corrections to info@it-ami.org and include "AMBOK Edit Feedback" in the subject line.

CONTENTS

LIST OF FIGURES

SECTION I

ARCHITECTURE MANAGEMENT FOUNDATION

Chapter 1

- Introduction

Chapter 2

- IT Architect Role

Chapter 3

- Architecture Management Office

CHAPTER 1

INTRODUCTION

The *Architecture Management Body of Knowledge (AMBOK™ Guide)* is a tool that contains a collection of standard definitions, processes, guidelines and frameworks that are generally accepted as best practices for the IT architecture management discipline. IT managers and professional architects can use the guide to help establish a consistent way for implementing IT architecture, locally and globally. Such guides have been widely used and accepted as a source of knowledge and as a reference guide for particular areas of interest. Examples include the use of *PMBOK® Guide* by the Project Management Institute (www.pmi.org) and the *KMBOK™* by the Knowledge Management Institute (www.kminstitute.org).

The *AMBOK™ Guide* is divided into two sections:
   1. The foundational aspects of architecture management
   2. The processes aspects of architecture management

This chapter will establish the first part of IT architecture management foundational knowledge. It is broken down as follows:

1.1 The IT-AMI Organization
1.2 Benefits of the *AMBOK™ Guide*
1.3 Historical View of Architecture
1.4 The Need for IT Architecture
1.5 What is IT Architecture?
1.6 Benefits of IT Architecture
1.7 Architecture Domains

1.1 The IT-AMI Organization

IT Architecture Management Institute Inc. also known as (Architecture Management Institute or AMI) is an organization focused on the education, research, publication, training and certification for IT architecture management. AMI's primary focus is to increase the awareness and importance of IT architecture so it becomes and continues to be an integral part of IT project delivery methodologies. AMI's establishment of the standards guide and supporting areas, such as research, education, and training for IT architects and managers, will increase the understanding of and adherence to IT architecture management concepts. The different architectural specializations such as systems architecture, software architecture, infrastructure architecture and others, can benefit from IT architecture management knowledge, including processes, models, and frameworks. This will build a consistent architecture understanding and implementation of IT projects.

Goals:

- Create common processes for establishing and implementing IT architectural project components and deliverables.
- Establish a clear definition of IT architecture and the role of an IT architect.
- Assist organizations in establishing and using the Architecture Management Office (AMO).
- Assist organizations in understanding how and when to engage IT architects.
- Assist organizations in understanding the career requirements, career paths, and development opportunities for IT architects.
- Act as a central source for collaboration, communication and publication for topics on IT architecture management.

Focus Areas:

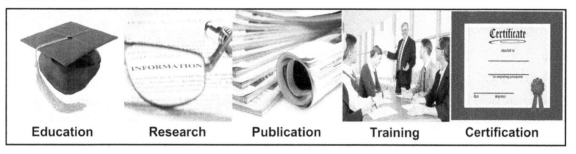

| Education | Research | Publication | Training | Certification |

Figure 1-1. Architecture Management Institute Focus Areas

1.1.1   Education

Education is an effective and important source for gaining and sharing knowledge. It provides a means for communicating important ideas, increasing one's ability to comprehend the topic being discussed, and allows for a way to promote, advance and share information. Education can take on different shapes and forms. AMI's approach is to share knowledge through multiple channels, including educational seminars, workshops, training courses, published research, white papers, and to publish articles in newsletters and magazines.

1.1.2   Research

Research is an essential component in advancing IT architecture management knowledge areas. Research builds the foundation for validating assumptions and providing a clear and tested method for increasing the knowledge segment being researched. AMI's initial research focus is related to the topic of IT architecture factors affecting the well know DeLone and McLean IS Success Model. Other research interests include the role of an IT architect, and the effect of IT architecture certification. AMI's growth as an organization will help expand its research focus to include other IT architecture related research topics.

1.1.3   Publication

Publication is a means of communicating with the general public and target audiences through the process of printing books, papers, and newsletters. Publication can also include electronic media such as eBooks, websites, digital newsletters, and various other digital means of communication. AMI's publication channels include but are not limited to books, such as the AMBOK™ Guide, electronic newsletters and information available on its website, and published articles.

1.1.4   Training

Training can entail different approaches to deliver knowledge through different channels, such as classroom training, online training, self-paced digital media training like visual DVD's or audio MP3's. AMI's training strategies emphasize the importance of starting with the basic foundational elements of IT architecture. AMI recommends that individuals who are new to IT architecture take the architecture foundation course to help them understand IT architecture management concepts before taking any advanced architecture specialization courses.

1.1.5   Certification

Certification is a process that affirms and certifies that an individual has met the criteria of required knowledge, education and experience necessary to achieve a specific certification designation. AMI currently has two certification designations: the Architecture Management Associate (AMA) and the Architecture Management Professional (AMP) certification. Check the AMI website for more details on the requirements and schedules.

1.2 Benefits of the AMBOK™ Guide

The *Architecture Management Body of Knowledge (AMBOK™ Guide)* is a tool that has a collection of standard definitions, processes, guidelines and frameworks that are generally accepted as best practices for the IT architecture management discipline. The guide can be used as a source of knowledge for managing, implementing and promoting IT architecture management practices. The guide can help organizations understand the architecture knowledge that is required to build strong architectural practices. A strong practice can lead to effective deployment of architecture techniques that will reduce IT operational costs and increase the project delivery success rate. The guide is a foundational starting point in the journey of IT architecture management and will continue to evolve and expand as more knowledge is acquired through research and industry project experience. The wide scope of architecture and the different views of architects make it difficult for this guide to be inclusive of all different areas. Feedback and contributions from IT architect professionals, organizations and researchers will add to the existing knowledge base and will contribute to the growth of this guide.

Key benefits of the AMBOK™ Guide include but are not limited to:

- Provides a consistent definition of common architecture terminologies, processes, and frameworks.

- A source for collecting, reviewing, and publishing IT architecture knowledge for architects to use.

- A central source for providing IT architects and managers with the foundational knowledge of IT architecture.

- Primary source for AMI's training materials.

- Primary source for AMI's certification exams.

1.3 Historical View of Architecture

Architecture from the physical structure and building design perspective is not new. It has roots dating back thousands of years, as seen in the coliseum in Rome and the pyramids in Egypt. Architecture can be defined as "Art + Discipline + Discipline." Art represents the physical appearance of a particular building. Art also represents the art of science, mathematics, and engineering that makes a person ask, how did they build such an iconic building? The first discipline represents the concept of a practice that uses processes, methodologies, frameworks, principles, and scientific theories to build such structures of engineering. The second discipline symbolizes the commitment and discipline to follow the rules of architectural practices.

Figure 1-2. A 72 AD ancient architecture (Coliseum, Rome)

INTRODUCTION

Looking at the ancient architecture, represented by the Coliseum in Figure 1-2, and modern day architecture, represented by the Burj Khalifa tower in Figure 1-3, people can begin to appreciate and respect architectural capabilities. These capabilities allowed an ancient structure, built in 72 AD, to withstand the test of time, and a modern architecture to be the tallest structure on earth standing 828 meters tall with 162 floors. There is no room for design errors. At this altitude, even a 1/2 inch offset in the walls or columns would mean a catastrophe.

By pausing for a moment and looking at both ancient architecture and modern architecture, a person really begins to think, they really have it figured out! How is it then that organizations are still struggling in trying to deliver Information Technology (IT) systems? Can they not learn from the architecture practices of building design and apply them to the information technology field, utilizing IT architecture?

Figure 1-3. A 2010 modern architecture (Burj Khalifa, Dubai)

1.4 The Need for IT Architecture

The need for IT architecture has been growing over the last two decades. Looking at the historic view of how information technology systems were developed, IT emerged as people began to replace paper based and manual processes. Computers were able to perform tasks and processes faster and cheaper, resulting in more process automation. However, initial use of technology did not have much of a systems design or architecture as we know it today. In effect, as organizations grow in size and processes become more complex, the dependency on technology and the need for proper design and architecture become accentuated. Large organizations realize that IT systems get out of control as they grow larger, and it is time to put in place IT architecture discipline to govern the way systems are implemented and managed. There is a point where one becomes so dependent on technology and absolutely needs IT architecture for running mission critical systems.

Figure 1-4. A 1948 vintage computer model using vacuum technology

Figure 1-4 shows a 1948 model for a stored computer program using vacuum tube technology. Figure 1-5 illustrates a modern day data centre, with rows of computer equipment, that has the capability to store and operate large systems. The bigger the operations the more advanced and complex these systems are. IT architecture consequently becomes required in order to handle the complexity of designing and building smarter systems.

Figure 1-5. Modern data centre computer equipment

Factors highlighting the need for IT architecture include but are not limited to:

- Effective management of complex systems.
- Cost reduction through standardization.
- Managing design risks.
- Proper documentation of systems.
- High level communication through architecture blueprints.
- Improving the systems quality.
- Increasing project delivery success through proper design.
- Managing systems complexity and scalability.

1.5 What is IT Architecture?

IT architecture in its generic form is defined as the art and science of designing and building information technology systems and other technology components such as hardware, software, application, network, infrastructure, security, data and information. The art and science components of IT architecture reflect the creativity of the design options and formally apply architecture processes, methodologies, tools, knowledge, frameworks, and principles. The outcome of IT architecture is a well designed system and/or technology components that meet the functional requirements and business needs.

IT Architecture can be described as but is not limited to:

- A set of principles, policies, models, frameworks and methodologies to govern how IT systems are implemented.

- A blueprint design for the underlying system, software, or hardware components.

- A method to enhance the effectiveness of system communication, using visual diagrams with different views to a variety of target audiences.

- A method to foster innovation by introducing new technology to the organization for competitive advantage.

- A method to document systems and technologies and record how these systems are designed and built.

- A method to link computer technology and business strategy through effective decision making processes and technology investments.

- A method to determine the impact of business decisions that require IT systems and its associated components changes.

- A method to help design, manage and maintain IT systems, data, applications, and the supporting infrastructure and technology components.

1.5.1   Components of IT Architecture

IT architecture consists of a number of components that are interrelated and work together to achieve the overall purpose of building the IT architecture concept. The components include but are not limited to the IT architect(s), a set of processes, frameworks, principles, standards, governance, documentation of artifacts, and a management office to oversee the architectural practices. The components are discussed in detail in Chapter 2 and Chapter 3.

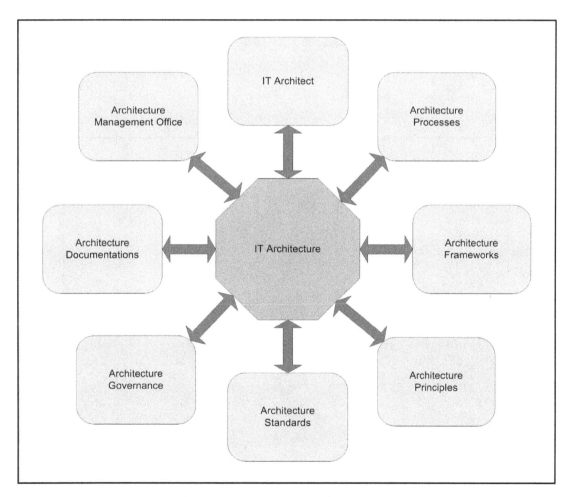

Figure 1-6. IT Architecture Components

I.5.2   IT Architecture vs. Building Architecture

By looking at and examining the concept of architecture from structure and building design, there is an apparent need to put a formal discipline to educate, govern and license individuals who want to become architects. Education components focus on the foundational knowledge required to be able to effectively design and build structures or buildings. This knowledge is then combined with internship experience accumulated by working under senior architects that guide new intern architects through real life projects. The third step requires a formal examination to test the individuals on the educational knowledge and how it can be applied to real work experience. The last step includes the licensing registration for individuals to be allowed to practice architecture.

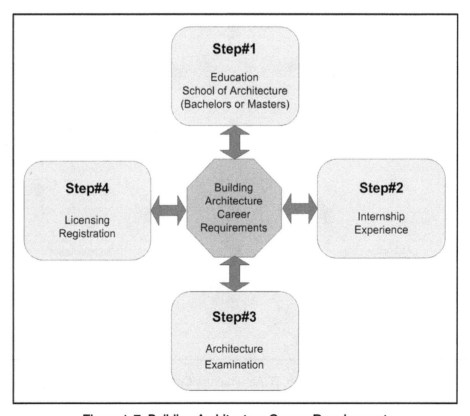

Figure I-7. Building Architecture Career Requirement

INTRODUCTION

Looking at architecture from an information technology perspective, there is an apparent need for setting up formal education, governance, and certification for IT architects who want to practice architecture in IT/IS departments. This will allow for a consistent way for IT architects to build future systems and technology implementations. However, IT architecture differs from building architecture in three areas. First is formal education. There is nowhere to date that provides a four or five year IT architect university degree similar to the one offered for building architecture. Second, there are no formal internship programs for IT architects such as the one required by the architects in building design. Third, there is no licensing or required certification designation to become a licensed IT architect similar to the one required by building architects. There are IT architect certification programs being offered, but they are not required by a government or an agency to give permission to IT architects to perform their duties. Figure 1-8 illustrates the current state of IT architecture career requirements.

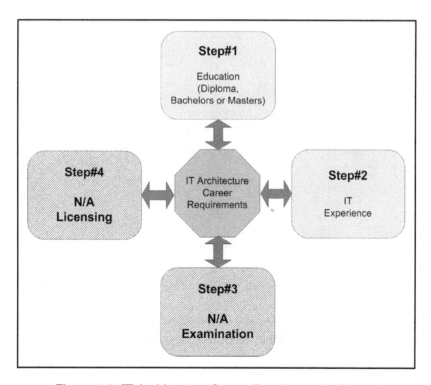

Figure 1-8. IT Architecture Career Requirement - Current

Figure I-9 illustrates where IT architecture career requirements should be transitioning to. First step is to strengthen the awareness that students interested in becoming IT architects need to have an IT related degree. Second step is to place emphasis on IT work related experience for solid understanding of what IT projects and lifecycles consist of, and how to design, develop and implement IT projects. Organizations need to invest in IT architecture training and education to move into a standard process and methodology of implementing IT architecture. Finally, there has to be a certification level that confirms the IT architect level of understanding of how to manage and implement architecture processes and techniques, combined with documented hours of architecture project experience necessary to attain a professional certification level.

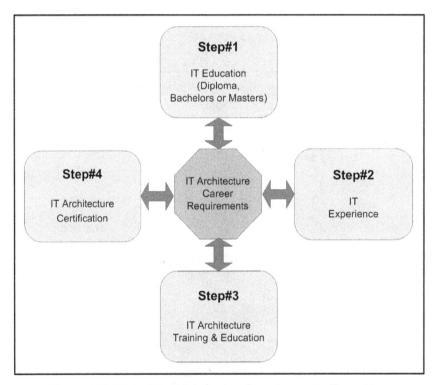

Figure I-9. IT Architecture Career Requirement - Transition

1.6 Benefits of IT Architecture

IT architecture value can be summarized in its ability to derive benefits for the business from its execution and implementation. IT architecture creates value by allowing organizations to make better decisions related to effectively leveraging time, money and resources. Architecture reduces the associated risk as proper design takes into consideration all the risks of the design options and how the risks can be mitigated. This makes organizations, large or small, more able to handle change, adapt to new environments, and become more efficient. Efficiency can be applied at the individual business unit and to the enterprise as a whole. As organizations grow in complexity, the business and technology environments become more difficult to manage, and harder to implement. Figure 1-10 illustrates some of the benefits of IT architecture not limited to: reduces risk, reduces cost, improves quality, drives integrity, manages complexity, fosters reuse, supports planning, seeks consensus, structural clarity, and supports impact analysis.

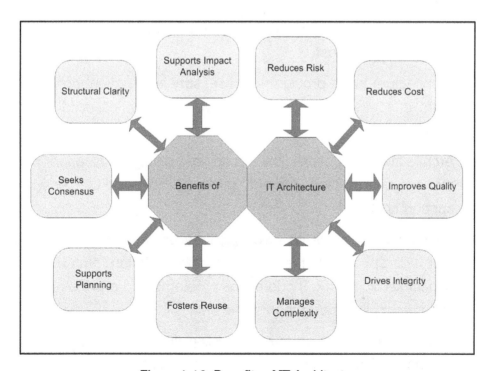

Figure 1-10. Benefits of IT Architecture

1.6.1 Reduces Risk

- Architecture examines the unknowns and asks the difficult questions to reduce the grey area between the known and the unknown.

- Architecture documents the risks, builds a plan to understand the risks, and provides alternatives for managing risks.

- Architecture leverages existing methods, patterns and frameworks that have been proven and tested to help reduce risks.

- Architecture builds contingency and backup design plans when unknowns are hard to plan or predict.

1.6.2 Reduces Cost

- Architecture allows organizations to think about system requirements and design principles ahead of time, hence reducing the risk of project delays, unforeseen infrastructure costs, resource requirements and design constraints before they happen.

- Architecture helps build reliable systems that will reduce maintenance and operational cost.

- Architecture helps provide the necessary information that will support more effective decisions, hence avoiding cost associated with bad decisions.

- Architecture focuses on building reliable, supportable and manageable systems through good design so it can ensure lower support costs.

- Architecture focuses on investing time up front to do proper design that will speed up the overall implementation time by avoiding unnecessary rework. It addresses problems and provides a resolution in the beginning rather than at the end.

- Architecture focuses on reusing existing components, technologies, and utilizing existing infrastructure services where possible to help reduce cost.

1.6.3 Improves Quality

- Architecture allows organizations to focus on system qualities such as reliability, adaptability, manageability, portability, scalability, security and service levels.

- Architecture promotes the reuse of institutional knowledge and project lessons learned at the enterprise level to improve system and implementation quality.

- Architecture avoids reactive decision making to business and technology changes without proper due diligence and planning to help reduce risk and improve quality.

- Architecture improves quality by avoiding the reinventing of the wheel and promotes the reuse of organizational knowledge, documented procedures, methods, standards, and infrastructure service.

1.6.4 Drives Integrity

- Architecture provides the ability to ask the question, "What if?" It anticipates the problems before they happen, irons out all the details and makes sure the "i's" are dotted and the "t's" are crossed before a single line of code is written.

- Architecture focuses on the interoperability of the communication methods taking place between systems and associated components to drive system integrity.

- Architecture improves system integrity through effective integration techniques for a wide range of computer systems, applications and platforms.

- Architecture focuses on balancing system integrity requirements and business needs through proper integration, using existing well established architecture methodologies.

1.6.5 Manages Complexity

- Architecture helps provide a simplistic view of the system by hiding its complexity and details.

- Architecture helps organizations go through the different architectural layers from a high level to a detailed level to check and validate decisions.

- Architecture focuses on the concept of simplification and the use of standards to reduce the number of choices that have not been tested.

- Architecture facilitates a repeatable and agreed upon decision making process.

- Architecture gives a holistic end-to-end view of the technology environments and the decision making processes to help avoid reactive untested decisions.

1.6.6 Fosters Reuse

- Architecture focuses on building reusable components that can be shared across the enterprise.

- Architecture implements hardware and software standards which can be used consistently across departments.

- Architecture helps reduce the siloed approach to IT implementation and leverages IT assets more efficiently and effectively.

- Architecture delivers solutions that are re-usable in a wide variety of ways to get the best Return On Investment (ROI) from implementations.

1.6.7   Supports Planning

- Architecture defines the building blocks and technical resource requirements.

- Architecture gives management the required system components to be used in the planning processes and project plans.

- Architecture improves business operations through the effective utilization of existing assets and planning processes.

- Architecture fosters business alignment through effective technology and business planning.

- Architecture guides business innovation through a systematic approach to introducing new technology to the environment and phasing out older technology from operations.

- Architecture acts as the compass guide for business and technology integration through effective technology road map design.

1.6.8   Seeks Consensus

- Architecture helps communicate the bigger picture to all stakeholders.

- Architecture allows for collaborative dialogue to make certain everyone is on the same page regarding the requirements, design, building and delivery of the system.

- Architecture lays down the facts and highlights the risks to make sure that everyone is up to speed on the design considerations.

1.6.9 Structural Clarity

- Architecture highlights the components of the system and makes them visible for discussion in the design process.
- Architecture gives management the ability to quickly determine requirements such as hardware, software, and resources.
- Architecture gives a high level view of the system design and how it interacts with existing IT assets.
- Architecture gives management the ability to make better decisions on how IT strategies will impact technology.

1.6.10 Supports Impact Analysis

- Architecture builds a dependency analysis within system components as well as upstream and downstream system integration.
- Architecture helps in the impact analysis of day-to-day troubleshooting, problem resolution and impact-to-scope changes.
- Architecture helps determine the cost and effort requirements for changes to the environment in its ability to understand the high level design, integration and dependencies between and within system components.

1.7 Architecture Domains

Architecture domains have unique requirements, knowledge and expertise represented as architecture areas of specialization. Such domains include business architecture, information architecture, application architecture, data architecture, solutions architecture, software architecture, systems architecture, infrastructure architecture, network architecture, hardware architecture, security architecture and enterprise architecture. IT architecture is a basic concept that defines common principles, framework, and methodologies that can be used by any one of the architecture specialization areas. Figure 1-11 illustrates 12 IT architecture domain areas for specialization.

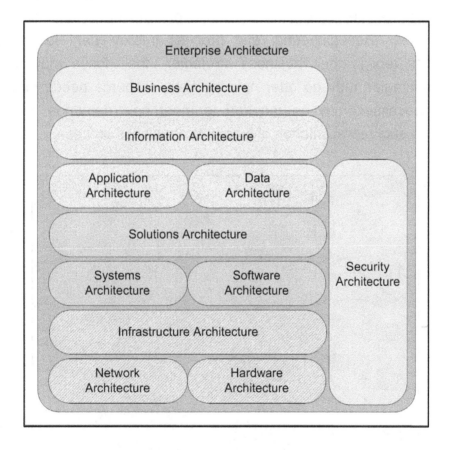

Figure 1-11. Architecture Domain Areas

1.7.1   Business Architecture

Business architecture focuses on taking an architectural approach to modeling business processes, models, people, structure, and operations. As business grows through global expansions, mergers and acquisitions as well as natural growth so does its business processes and models. This results in more complex business processes, models and operations that need to be architected. Business architecture takes a step back to view and understand the organization's core businesses, processes and operational needs.   Using a visual representation and the use of drawings helps map the business processes and their interactions and identifies opportunities for improvements. Business architecture leverages techniques and methods such as Lean Six Sigma, Process Reengineering, and process improvement techniques. As organizations realign their business strategies, their focus may shift, their business strategies may go after new markets, resource needs may change and new processes may be required to meet new demands. Figure 1-12 illustrates a visual representation of a complex business process.

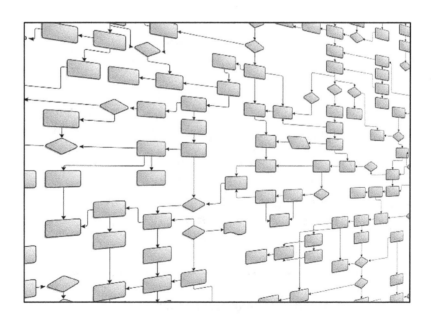

Figure 1-12. Business Architecture Illustration

I.7.2   Information Architecture

Information architecture focuses on how organizations can structure, categorize and organize their information in an easy and consumable fashion. Information can be a source of wealth for organizations to harness through proper information architecture techniques. Information that exists but is inaccessible is useless to organizational growth. However, if it is very well organized and accessible to executives, managers and frontline staff, information becomes a strategic and competitive advantage. Organizations are living in the information age and information needs to be properly architected to determine the best approach for managing, organizing and accessing. A common use of information architecture is seen in libraries as they are required to organize, categorize and manage the wealth of information and knowledge in an accessible and simple way. People can find books, novels, and magazines using a fast, accurate and easy method. Information architecture does not look at how the information is physically stored. This will be discussed in data architecture. Figure I-13A illustrates what type of information is required on a website. Figure I-13B illustrates how content and information should be organized and placed on a website to provide easy and fast access to information.

Figure I-13A. What Information Is Required   Figure I-13B. How Information Is Organized

I.7.3   Application Architecture

Application architecture focuses on how organizational business requirements and processes can be satisfied with a series of applications that are integrated to fulfill specific needs. Applications can be purchased, customized, or built from scratch to meet business requirements. Application architecture maps the inventory of applications to the business processes and functional areas to determine their integration needs, backend systems and hardware requirements. Applications can be very small, such as the applications built for mobile devices. Or they can be large ones that process complex business rules and processes. Figure I-14 illustrates a list of applications that are used for mobile devices such as calendar, chat, email, and photo.

Figure I-14. Applications for Mobile Devices

1.7.4   Data Architecture

Data architecture focuses on how data will be defined, stored, and managed at the conceptual, logical and physical layers of the database management systems. The actions, interfaces, and access to data are defined by data architecture. Data architects examine the data elements that need to be stored and determine the best approach for storing, retrieving and manipulating data in the most efficient and effective way. The integrity of the data, the speed of data access, the data sizing requirements and the best data modeling techniques to be used will be determined by the data architect. Figure 1-15 illustrates a data model depicting how data will be stored in a set of tables with their associated relationships.

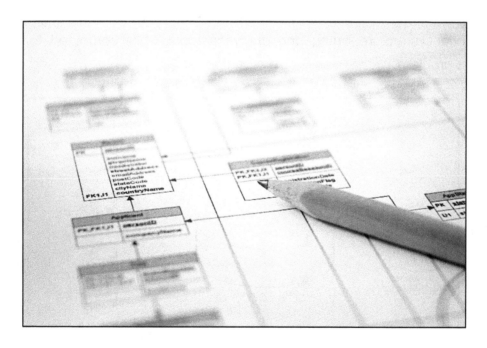

Figure 1-15. A Data Model for a System

I.7.5   Solutions Architecture

Solutions architecture focuses on delivering creative solutions for business problems that may span multiple technology domains. Solutions architecture may leverage software packages, systems, applications and infrastructure components to solve a business problem. It may span broad technology specialization and views the other architecture domains as tools that contribute to the solution set for the problem being addressed. Solutions architecture includes both the internal and external structures and behavior of the solutions set. Internal structure includes how the components and sub-components of a particular system will work together. External structure includes the integration requirement to make the systems, applications and software components, that are interconnected, work together to deliver the overall solution. Figure I-16 illustrates a data warehouse solution architecture diagram depicting how multiple solutions such as a database system, ETL components, business intelligence system, reporting and analytics tools, are combined to solve a business problem.

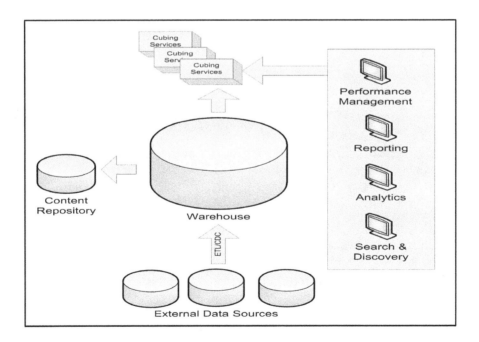

Figure I-16. Data Warehouse Solution Architecture

I.7.6   Systems Architecture

Systems architecture focuses on determining the components and structures that make up the system and how these structures are linked and integrated with each other. Systems architecture defines the behavior between the components to clearly articulate how the components need to react to actions and functions that are executed within the systems' boundaries. Systems architecture leverages multiple views to depict how the system components work with one other. Systems architecture may include hardware, software and infrastructure components that make up the overall system architecture design. Organizations may decide to build systems that are unique to their business needs instead of purchasing applications or software packages. Building a system for an organization requires good understanding of the business processes and domain knowledge expertise to help address the system's design. Figure I-17 illustrates a systems architecture diagram depicting components of an e-commerce system.

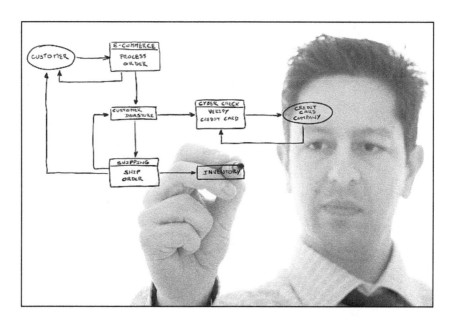

Figure I-17. Systems Architecture Illustration

1.7.7   Software Architecture

Software architecture focuses on building software that contains a set of programs, instructions, logic, interfaces, data and documentation that provides a means of interaction with a computer system. Software can be embedded into hardware components, operating system level components, or utility based software components. Software architecture is used heavily by software companies as they are in the business of building software packages that can be sold to clients. Organizations may have research and development units that use in-house software architecture practices. However, most government organizations, financial institutions, banks, insurance and other companies tend to focus more on solutions, applications or systems architecture instead of software architecture. Figure 1-18 illustrates a software architecture diagram depicting how the components of a software program are designed.

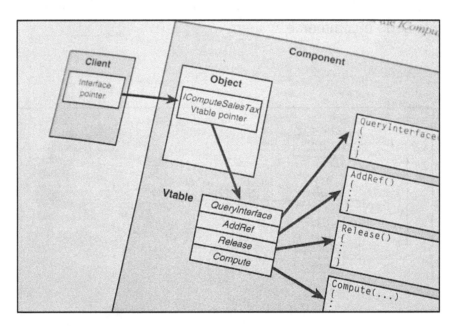

Figure 1-18. Software Architecture Illustration

I.7.8 Infrastructure Architecture

Infrastructure architecture focuses on the core IT components that include hardware, software and service required to support the day-to-day operations of an enterprise. These components include but are not limited to the network, telecommunication, data centre, data stores, data management components, hardware components, servers, operating systems, enterprise systems, internet connectivity, email, and consulting services. Infrastructure architecture plays a critical role in figuring out how all the IT infrastructure components are going to get connected and work together seamlessly. Infrastructure architecture is responsible for how the introduction of new technology and phasing out older technology will occur with minimal risk to the organization. Figure I-19 illustrates a data centre with infrastructure components supporting an organization's technology needs.

Figure I-19. Data Centre Infrastructure Components

I.7.9 Network Architecture

Network architecture focuses on the logical and physical network components that need to be architected to support the communication needs of the enterprise. Network architecture may include but is not limited to Wide Area Network (WAN), Local Area Network (LAN), Virtual Private Network (VPN), internet, intranet, switches, servers, security, routers, firewalls, wireless technologies and cores. Figure I-20 illustrates a sample network architecture diagram depicting how network components are connected.

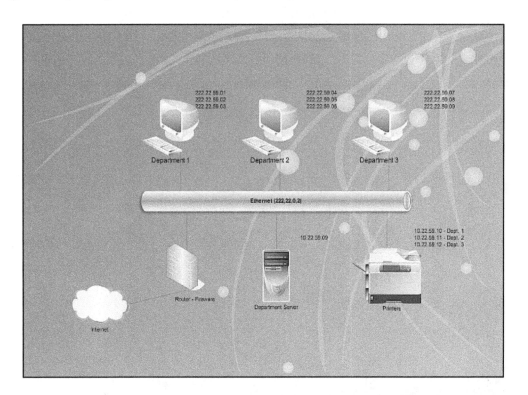

Figure I-20. Network Architecture Illustration

1.7.10   Hardware Architecture

Hardware architecture focuses on physical hardware components and their relationship to the overall system design. Hardware components can include but are not limited to server rack components, computer housing, networking devices, motherboards, CPU's, Power supply, RAM, BIOS, USB, SCSI, CD, DVD. The hardware architecture domain is mostly associated with hardware vendors that spend a great deal of time designing and architecting new hardware technologies that push the speed of processing and storage capabilities. Figure 1-21 illustrates components of a personal computer and the associated wiring diagrams.

Figure 1-21. Hardware Components Illustration

1.7.11   Security Architecture

Security architecture focuses on the security measures that are required to protect the enterprise from threats while maintaining the flexibility and efficiency of conducting day-to-day business activities. It is a constant juggling act for security architects to tighten or loosen security measures—to find the right balance between security and flexibility without compromising the security controls. Security architecture includes but is not limited to authentication, authorizing, intrusion detection, firewalls, encryption, antivirus protection from malicious software, hacking and cyber vandalism protection, identity theft protection, auditing and control processes. Figure 1-22 illustrates how access to computer systems is protected from the outside world behind a security firewall.

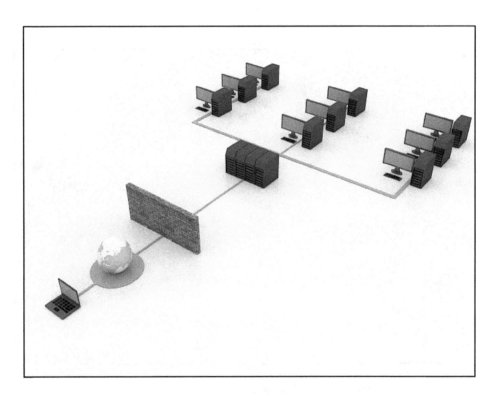

Figure 1-22. Security Diagram with a Firewall Illustration

I.7.I2   Enterprise Architecture

Enterprise Architecture (EA) focuses on the IT architecture of the entire enterprise by linking business strategy and technology capabilities. There are well established EA frameworks such as the Zachman Framework for Enterprise Architecture, TOGAF, and the FEA. These frameworks describe all the major components of an EA and have been very well documented. The scope of Enterprise Architecture includes all the architecture domains specializations that have been discussed previously. The enterprise architect who leads the enterprise architecture spends a great deal of time working with IT and business executives to understand the business strategies and corporate direction. Once the business strategies are understood, IT infrastructure components, systems, applications and data need to be mapped out in order to identify technology gaps. Technology roadmaps, including both tactical and strategic projects, are required to close the gaps between the business strategies and technology, resulting in the alignment between business and IT. Figure I-23 illustrates an example of global view of technology.

Figure I-23. Enterprise Architecture Illustration

CHAPTER 2

IT ARCHITECT ROLE

The IT architect role plays an important part of the IT department technical leadership team. IT architects are considered technology leaders who have the ability to share the deep understanding of the technology domains as well as the management responsibilities through the empowerment of their leadership abilities. IT architects share similar roles and accountabilities as architects from structural and building design. They are accountable for the overall design of the particular object or system. They are responsible for the management of the architecture lifecycle and the leadership vision to spearhead initiatives and lead a strong team with varied skills and domain expertise.

This chapter will establish the second part of the foundational knowledge by understanding the IT architect role and how it benefits organizations. This section is broken down as follows:

2.1 IT Architect Overview

2.2 IT Architect Responsibilities

2.3 IT Architect Skills

2.4 IT Architect Education

2.5 IT Architect Competency Framework

2.6 Architect Title Variations

2.7 IT Architect Career Levels

2.1 IT Architect Overview

IT architects are considered technology leaders with strong technical and non-technical skills. Established architects have a strong experience base in architecting many projects and large systems that gained them the knowledge and expertise in full lifecycle architecture delivery. The architect's experience is measured by how many projects they have built, how big the projects were, how complicated were the design patterns, and how they identified and solved problems. Architects need to have strong leadership skills to be the go-to person for design considerations and problem resolution. This requires strong analytical and problem solving skills; skills which allow architects to think outside the box and recommend solutions that span project boundaries. Taking ownership and leading initiatives such as problem identification, proof of technology and vendor product analysis are key skills in the architect's toolbox.

Figure 2-1. IT Architect Vision and Scope

As technology leaders of a project, architects work with many groups. The way they manage and handle relationships is considered a key success factor in building an architecture that can be delivered on time and within budget. Good architects have a solid relationship with many people such as systems analysts, developers, management, and technical staff to ensure that system components are coordinated and will fit together properly. Building a team culture through relationships will strengthen the coordination and effectiveness of the team. Knowing when to use these relationships will give a stronger foundation for effective negotiations that will create a win-win situation for everyone. Leveraging the push and pull negotiation technique to guarantee project delivery is an accountability of architects.

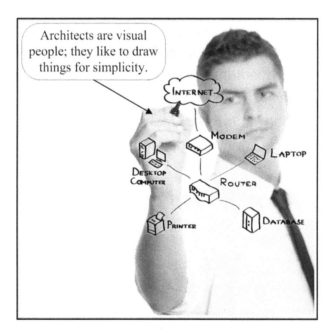

Figure 2-2. IT Architect Personality

Technical skills can vary between IT architects, some may have a focus on security, data, application, software, information, infrastructure, or networking. The broader the technical skills, the more flexible the architects become. Architects understand the business domain and knowing how the system will benefit the organization will help link the technology and the business value of the system. In order to stay on top of technology trends, architects have to participate in a continuous learning cycle and be willing to adapt to change.

Technology keeps changing; new design patterns are emerging; knowing how things got done in the past and where they need to go in the future is a strategic thought process required by architects. Architects are accountable for technology decision-making in projects by documenting the advantages and disadvantages of the objects being evaluated. Architects must plan and organize what needs to be built by breaking a system into its component parts, feeding the project management methodology with the required resources and the dependency analysis, thus making for a successful project delivery. Effective communication can also make or break an architect. Without communication, architects cannot lead, negotiate, or build strong relationships.

2.2 IT Architect Responsibilities

IT architect responsibilities span a wide range of accountabilities depending on the role they play. However, a common denominator between the different roles includes the ability to lead projects as technical experts—the ability to manage technical components, relationships, and resources, and the responsibility to acquire deep and broad technical knowledge, experience, and expertise. This enables architects to make effective decisions, design complex solutions and be the go-to person for technical and domain knowledge. The architect's knowledge of how systems are designed, assembled, integrated and built empowers team members and allows them to tap into the architect's knowledge base.

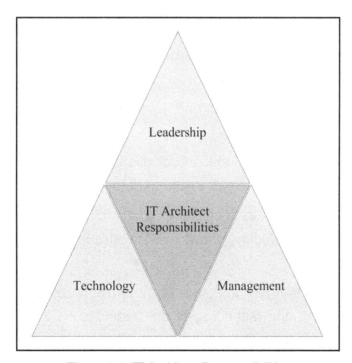

Figure 2-3. IT Architect Responsibilities

2.2.1 Leadership Responsibilities

- Provide leadership in promoting architectural vision, strategy, and principles.

- Provide leadership in understanding business and technical domains.

- Provide leadership in developing a vision on how the systems are going to deliver value and satisfy business needs.

- Provide leadership in guidance for developing and implementing systems within identified constraints.

- Provide leadership in developing a vision on how systems are going to be designed, assembled and built, and communicate it to the different audiences, including stakeholders and development teams.

- Provide leadership in understanding the depth, breadth, opportunities and limitations of the technology being implemented.

- Provide leadership by inspiring, mentoring, and encouraging the project team to think outside the box and develop best practices and alternatives for solving problems.

- Provide leadership for architectural alignment between business needs and technology capabilities for implementation efforts.

- Provide leadership in gathering architectural requirements, design artifacts, and conducting interviews to streamline and identify design gaps.

- Provide leadership in keeping up with technology trends and what products, tools, and technologies are available on the market today and what will be available in the future.

- Provide leadership in modeling the proposed solution and identifying any constraints that are internally or externally imposed on the design.

- Provide leadership in communication, facilitating conflict resolution between different groups, and moderating and promoting consensus within project design.

2.2.2 Management Responsibilities

- Manage the technical voice and communication strategies for the project team.

- Manage translation of business requirements into high level and detailed design documents.

- Manage architectural frameworks that provide a cost effective and easy way to implement manageable, scalable, portable and high performance architecture design.

- Manage and implement standards and policies for the organization's architectural initiatives.

- Create and manage IT roadmaps that are closely aligned with the IT executives' strategies and vision.

- Manage the governance processes, including decision approval and signoff authority on architecture deliverables.

- Manage business and IT expectations by acting as a liaison between the business department and IT staff.

- Manage technology selections, including hardware, software and services.

- Manage the architecture lifecycle and integrate it with other methodologies such as the software development lifecycle.

- Manage and monitor development initiatives in accordance with the selected architecture blueprints created during the design, build and test phases.

- Manage stakeholders' expectations and know when to say yes and when to hold back and say no for the benefit of the project.

- Manage the risk associated with things that are outside of the architect's control.

2.2.3　Technical Responsibilities

- Provide a technical overview of the entire system and how the components and subcomponents are designed, integrated, and linked to help guide design decisions.

- Provide technical awareness of emerging trends in technology that could impact existing projects and future project direction.

- Provide support and participation to internal and external standards organizations and industry groups to help influence and advance technology trends and best practices.

- Provide technical oversight for products, tools, software, hardware and vendor evaluation and selection.

- Provide technical expertise and guidance on systems and environments integration.

- Provide expertise in creating and delivering technical presentations to different audiences, both technical and non technical.

- Provide high level technical and design consultation to team members.

- Provide technical recommendations on how to meet both short and long term strategies.

- Provide technical strategies for phasing out legacy systems, integrating existing systems, and introducing new technologies to the environment.

- Provide technical expertise in handling changes to the environment and leveraging the appropriate strategies to mitigate the risk associated with change.

- Provide technical documentation that describes the entire system interaction at a high level, through the use of architectural blueprints and diagrams.

- Provide technical decisions for evaluating alternatives and highlighting the advantages and disadvantages of each alternative.

2.3 IT Architect Skills

IT architects are considered technology leaders that have strong technical skills and non technical skills such as people skills, management skills and business skills. Architects must satisfy high expectations and accountabilities and require a vast, well rounded skills set to meet the requirements for leading projects. It takes years and many project implementation experiences to master many of the required skills. Organizations need to establish a strong architecture career plan to make sure that the skills are being developed, tuned and mastered over time. Each individual architect has a different personal dynamic and likely have unique skill strengths and weaknesses.

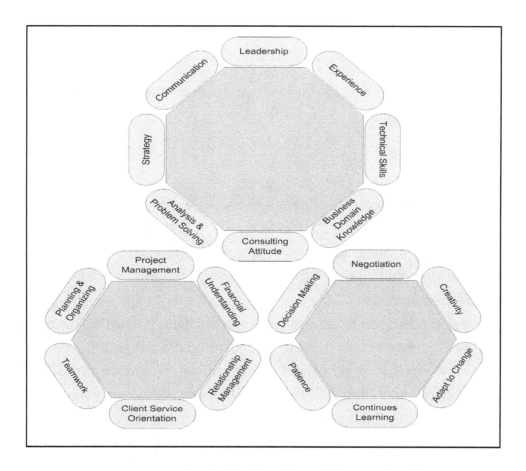

Figure 2-4. IT Architect Skills

2.3.1   Leadership

- Architects need to have passion for technology and, to an extent, act as a technology evangelist.
- Architects need to have strong leadership skills that are earned through knowledge, wisdom, experience and contribution to the technical community.
- Architects need to be able to mentor people around them and build knowledge through sharing ideas, experiences and coaching.
- Architects need to understand their own strengths and weaknesses and need to be humble with regard to what they know and honest about what they do not know.
- Architects need to be open minded to support or challenge new ideas.
- Architects need to be true leaders that can talk the talk and walk the walk.

2.3.2   Experience

- Architects need to have extensive experience in implementing architecture on projects that vary in size and complexity.
- Architects need to have trust and credibility in their architecture design that can be backed by prior, successful project implementations.
- Architects need to have experience in taking calculated risks and not be afraid to try new things (depending on the risk level) even though it may result in a perceived failure. Failure improves one's ability to understand that what they have attempted does not work; it is a step forward in the quest for research and innovation.
- Architects need to have experience in participating in knowledge sharing events. They should have attended architecture training and

have an interest in pursuing some type of architecture certification in the future.

- Architects need to have strong design experience and the ability to view design considerations from multiple angles.

2.3.3   Technical Skills

- Architects need to have deep technical knowledge in the areas that they specialize in as well as a broad general knowledge of other technology domains.
- Architects need to understand methodologies such as the Software Development Life Cycle (SDLC), Unified Modeling Language (UML), Rational Unified Processes (RUP) and others.
- Architects need to understand both functional and non-functional requirements such as performance, scalability, reliability, manageability, interoperability and supportability.
- Architects need to understand the different layers of design such as application layer, middle-tier, and backend components.
- Architects need to understand how the information and data will be managed, stored, retrieved, and manipulated.
- Architects need to understand technical components such as network, hardware, servers, and security, and how they impact system design.

2.3.4   Business Domain Knowledge

- Architects need to understand the business domain of the areas they are responsible for.
- Architects need to be very clear on what the business expectations are and how these expectations can be translated and transformed to achievable results.

- Architects need to speak business language, terminology, acronyms and policies to understand a business problem and determine how it can be solved.
- Architects need to look for cross domain knowledge when solving problems to have a bigger view of how problems have been solved in other business domains areas.

2.3.5 Consulting Attitude

- Architects need to have a consulting mind and attitude as they play a key role in leading projects.
- Architects can take on multiple roles on projects as consultants, advisors and technical knowledge sources. They contribute their expertise and support to the success of a project.
- Architects need to be trusted and well respected in their domain consulting expertise.

2.3.6 Analysis & Problem Solving

- Architects need to have analysis and problem solving skills, having demonstrated the ability to solve complex problems.
- Architects need to be able to look at the problems from multiple viewpoints to be able to perform detailed analysis and come up with a recommended approach for solving complex problems.
- Architects need to have the characteristics of a detective. They must collect and document the facts. They need to view the business problem from multiple angles, including a neutral perspective. They must determine the tools available on hand and then evaluate which tool should be used, based on factors such as cost, time and appropriateness.

2.3.7   Strategy

- Architects need to have a strategic focused mind to be able to translate business strategies to real life systems that can deliver value.
- Architects need to understand both long term and short term strategies and use architectural roadmaps to capture, plan and monitor initiatives.
- Architects need to understand how their strategic thinking will be leveraged to make architecting future strategic systems a reality.

2.3.8   Communication

- Architects' key strength relies on their ability to communicate effectively to different audiences.
- Architects must have the ability to understand deep and complex technical knowledge that then can be abstracted and summarized to management and executives in an easy and understandable format.
- Architects need to demonstrate excellent communication skills to include written, verbal, and presentational.
- Architects need to think on their feet and adjust the way they communicate based on the audience's ability to understand technical and business terms.
- Architects need to have creative presentation skills that can be used as tools for good communication strategies.

2.3.9   Project Management

- Architects need to understand the project management methodology and how it integrates with the architecture management processes.
- Architects work very closely with the project manager as their project leadership counterpart.

- Architects assist project managers with the work breakdown structure to include the technical components, subcomponents and their dependencies.
- Architects help feed the project management risk identification process with the technical and design risks that need to be documented and managed.
- Architects help feed project cost estimation for hardware, software and development efforts required to complete the project.

2.3.10 Financial Understanding

- Architects need to have financial understanding of how IT budgets, hardware costs, equipment leases and project estimations operate.
- Architects are sometimes required to support decisions with ROI calculations to determine technology directions and investment opportunities.
- Architects work very closely with project managers to define project estimations for technology and delivery time expectations that translate into financial reporting.
- Architects need to understand the bill of materials that are required to implement the architecture, including all the associated costs in hardware, software, and resources.
- Architects need to have a good understanding of the different budgetary, financial allocations such as capital, operational and strategic budgets and how each project component can be mapped to the appropriate budget plan.

2.3.11 Relationship Management

- Architects need to play a role in building strong relationships with technical and non technical team members, managers, executives and external technical community.

- Architects need to be able to influence through their relationships with people.
- Architects need to use their relationship management expertise to assist in conflict resolution.
- Architects need to be able to use their negotiation skills combined with their relationship management skills to bring project members, stakeholders and external influences to consensus to help increase the success rate of project delivery.

2.3.12 Client Service Orientation

- Architects need to think, act and implement a service mentality as they view the users of the system as clients who are looking for technology services to meet their business needs.
- Architects need to look beyond the technical domain of the implementation and view the entire process from the client's view and determine if there are areas of improvement that need to be incorporated in the design.
- Architects need to think and treat clients as if they were seeking services of their own.

2.3.13 Teamwork

- Architects need to be strong team players to be able to work with different team members such as project managers, systems analysts, business analysts, developers, and testers.
- Architects teamwork composition tends to be wide in scope. It requires a strong ability to handle different expectations from different team members and to be able to communicate and build a strong teamwork atmosphere and spirit.

2.3.14 Planning & Organizing

- Architects need to have effective and efficient planning methods to be able to execute on project deliverables.
- Architects need to be well organized and detailed to make sure the overall integrity of the design is intact through proper documentation and following a well defined process and methodology.
- Architects start from a high level concept of architecture which will then will be broken down to manageable components that are organized and categorized for the building process.
- Architects need to validate and execute the architecture plan based on the best approach that has been tested and proved to yield the greatest value for the project.
- Architects need to understand and participate in different levels of planning, including strategic planning, IS planning and technology planning, depending on the role and scope.
- Architects need to plan and organize the system's building blocks and material required for the project. Architects need to understand when and how each part will be executed and connected with other components.

2.3.15 Negotiation

- Architects need to be strong negotiators, have a diplomatic spirit, and posses the required negotiation techniques that are mandated by the job.
- Architects need to exercise their negotiation skills when balancing design considerations with business requirements and technology challenges.
- Architects seek mutual cooperation for a win-win situation between the architect deliverables and stakeholder requirements.

- Architects are under constant pressure to deliver more, faster, and cheaper, which requires good negotiation skills between different groups to make it happen.
- Architects need to know how to deal with difficult situations, including dealing with people who have a strong resistance to change.

2.3.16 Creativity

- Architects need to have a sense of art and creativity to be able to implement effective a simple architecture design that can solve complex business problems in the fewest steps.
- Architects need a broad view of how to use tools and technology to solve problems and be able to test the limits of the capabilities that are available.
- Architects need to have the ability to manage complexity through creative thinking and adaptability.
- Architects need to be able to acknowledge that every problem has a solution, and it is how an individual goes about solving such problems that will create the basis for creativity.
- Architects need to be artistic in their design, especially if they are building applications that are customer facing. Hiding the complexity and introducing elegancy is an art.

2.3.17 Adapt to Change

- Architects need to have a strong desire to adapt to the different environments and must believe that change is inevitable.
- Architects need to balance change demands in requirements, tools, technology and resources.
- Architects need to adapt to change through effective management techniques and risk mitigation.

- Architects need to build flexible architecture to handle unforeseen changes with the lowest impact to the project and environment.
- Architects need to understand that there is a high rate of change in technological environments, and they need to adjust and change with what the future may bring.

2.3.18 Continues Learning

- Architects need to be open to lifelong learning to keep up with the rapid changes in technology.
- Architects need to handle different types of learning media such as online learning, computer based training, product or vendor specific training, self-teaching through reading books, journals, websites, blogs and email news.
- Architects need to be active by participating in conferences and knowledge sharing events.
- Architects need to be able to incorporate newly learned material into existing processes to help improve and advance architectural practices.

2.3.19 Patience

- Architects need to be very patient and handle tough conditions and choices.
- Architects need to be patient in times of constant change and turbulence.
- Architects have to stay relaxed, re-calculate design options, continue to mitigate risks and take charge by pushing the overall project progress forward.
- Architects need to be patient to be able to collect all the business requirements and pay close attention to details to make sure all design options have been addressed.

- Architects need to be patient when trying to explain very technical concepts to non technical people. They have to come up with ways to reduce complexity and adapt to the target audience.
- Architects need to be patient when dealing with people that always like to make things harder than what they need to be.
- Architects need to be patient with external legislative regulations and government agencies, since designs may have to change based on new regulatory requirements that are typically driven by hard dates.

2.3.20 Decision Making

- Architects need to make effective decisions based on wise judgment, experience and integrity.
- Architects need to execute critical reasoning in order to make the best decision for the organization.
- Architects use the decision alternative process to conduct analysis and document the alternatives. This will help determine the best choice for the organization.

2.4 IT Architect Education

IT architecture education from a full Bachelor's degree or Master's programs does not exist to date. Using the architecture concept from building design, there are Bachelor's, Master's and PhD programs that are dedicated to understanding, teaching and researching architecture. Among them are Cornell College of Architecture, Art and Planning, and MIT department of Architecture. However, there is some progress in the field of software architecture in that it is being offered as a concentration area in some IT Bachelor's degrees. There is, nevertheless, no overarching formal IT architecture education such as seen in architecture of building design. This creates a number of pockets where educational training and some certification programs have been investing in building a knowledge base to fill the formal educational gap that exists today.

Knowing that there is a gap in formal IT architecture education makes for a big variation in the existing, professional IT architects' educational backgrounds. Some architects may have computer science, mathematics, software engineering, information systems and other IT related education. Furthermore, there are IT architects that have non IT or technical degrees such as English, history, and management. They have learned IT architecture the hard way by learning on the job and painstakingly gaining work experience in designing systems. It will be beneficial to build IT architecture educational programs and internship experiences for IT architects. It is highly recommended that architects have IT or related fields educational background to establish a strong foundation for their IT architect career.

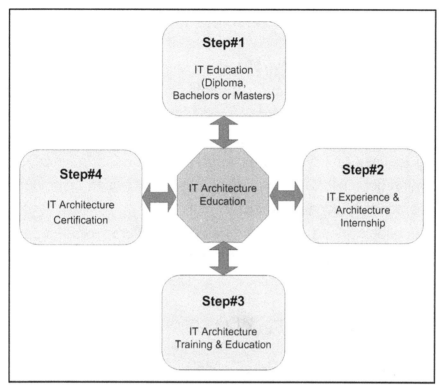

Figure 2-5. IT Architect Education

2.4.1   University/College IT Education

- Architects need to have a formal university or college education that has a strong basis in IT or related areas such as, but not limited to, computer science, software engineering, information systems, information technology or computer engineering.
- Architects need to look at pursuing advanced degrees such as graduate education in IT, computer science, or business with focus on IT to help advance their architecture career.

2.4.2   IT Experience & Architecture Internship

- Architects need to have IT related technical experiences.
- Architects need to have completed a formal internship to gain work experience in implementing architecture projects through guidance from more senior architects. This allows the architectural practice guidelines and procedures to be understood by new architects. This will reduce risk since final design approval has to be signed off by the senior architect guiding the project.
- Architects need to track their architecture experience hours on projects to help them towards their career advancement and future certification requirements.

2.4.3   IT Architect Training & Education

- Architects need to stay up to date on technology trends and should take advantage of training opportunities in architecture, tools, technology, and product design.
- Architects need to contribute to the growth of the architectural practices by training others through knowledge sharing and training sessions.

2.4.4   IT Architect Certification

- Architects need to work towards a certification program that will evaluate their architecture knowledge as well as processes and methodologies.
- Architects need to seek certification credentials that will be based on a standard knowledge base to gain career advancement opportunities and recognition.

2.5 IT Architect Competency Framework

The IT architect competency framework illustrated in Figure 2-6 represents a set of key competency areas that make up the architect's DNA. At first glance, the competency framework may seem overwhelming, but with proper planning and career development opportunities, organizations can build their future architectural staffing needs. The level of competency expertise required for each architect level will be discussed in section 2.7. The framework's foundation is based on architecture experience. Its focus is on communication, leadership and strategy, and the core is made up of 16 competency areas.

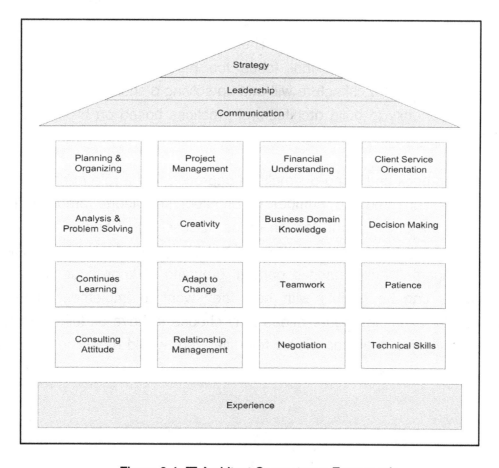

Figure 2-6. IT Architect Competency Framework

2.6 Architect Title Variations

Architects strive to achieve simplicity in the design even though sometimes the object being architected is very complex in nature. Taking complex things and transforming them to smaller, manageable and simpler designs is an art. The IT industry dynamics has contributed significantly to changes in roles, titles and required experience for IT individuals. The IT architect role is no different; industry has created so many title variations for architects that it is making Human Resources (HR) departments struggle to keep up with the different titles, role definitions and compensation. There are many cases where we see the word "architect" placed after technical, products, platform or technology specific names such as, ".Net Architect," "MS Exchange Architect," "Java Architect," and "PeopleSoft Architect." There is very little consistency in role and title definition. Organizations that focus too much on a specific solution, technology, or field of architecture will end up solving a short term need but will miss the opportunity to build architectural practices based on broad resource capability.

Taking a step back and using a simplified approach to the role of an architect, organizations can create a number of architect knowledge areas that are aligned with the architectural domain areas discussed in Chapter I. This will restrict adding the word architect after technology specific tools or technology. The list in figure 2-7 illustrates a general grouping of knowledge areas, but organizations can be flexible with how they want to implement such title variations. For example, organizations may choose to have all their architects titled IT Architect or they can pick a few titles that would meet their business needs.

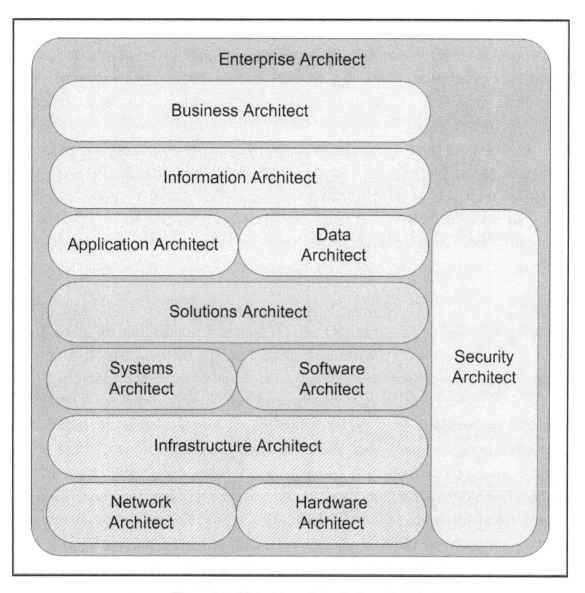

Figure 2-7. IT Architect Domain Specific Titles

2.7 IT Architect Career Levels

Architect levels vary depending on how big and mature the organization's architectural practice is. There are typically four levels, starting with the first level of IT architect or its role variation equivalents: systems architect, application architect, or network architect. The second level is senior IT architect. The third level is portfolio or program architect—if the organization is large enough to be running program and portfolios. The fourth level is enterprise architect or chief architect, responsible for the organization's enterprise wide architecture. Large organizations may have a fifth level, dedicated to chief architects, who may have a number of enterprise architects reporting to them. This is based on the size and scope of the architecture practice.

The junior or intermediate titles of an IT architect should not be used by organizations as architects are strong technical people that typically have been performing at a senior level in other technical areas of the organization before moving into architecture. A common progression is seen from the software development perspective: those who become senior developers or technical leads often decide to make the choice to move up to architecture. There are factors such as ability, dynamics, project opportunities, complexity of projects, and how much an organization invests in architecture that influence how fast an individual can move up in their architecture career. For example, someone might be an architect in an organization but did not have the opportunity to architect many projects compared with a more active organization. AMI's architecture competency framework can provide guidance to help organizations build their own map of how the IT architect progression will be established.

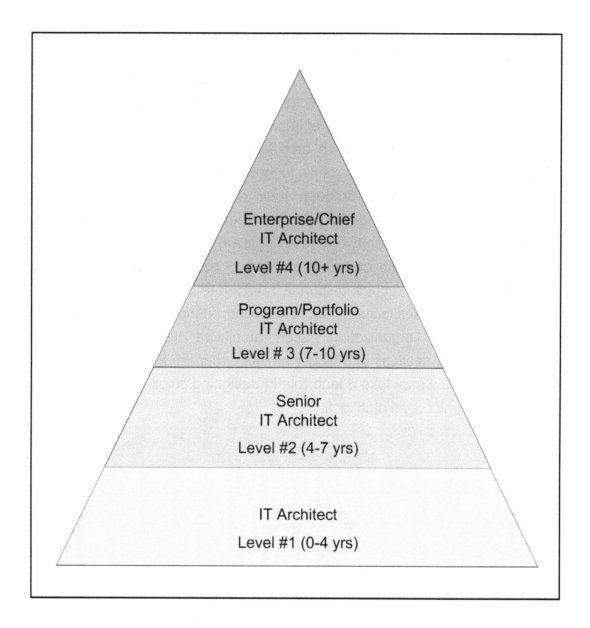

Figure 2-8. IT Architect Career Levels

2.7.I   IT Architect Level

Architects are a senior level resource. The first level in architecture covers new architects who might not have any architecture experience and architects who might have up to four years of architecture experience. This assumes that new architects are already at a senior level in other technical areas before moving to architecture. For example, network architects may have started as network technicians and moved up the ranks to become senior network specialists. They may have wanted to broaden their horizons and become network architects responsible for the entire process of designing and building networks. Another example would be software developers who moved up in their career to senior software developers and then decided to become software architects. Architects at this level require guidance from more senior architects to help them through the architecture processes and standards that have been established by the organization. Such architects typically take part in architecting smaller sections of a bigger project under the lead of a more senior level architect. They may take a lead role in designing smaller projects that are reviewed by a senior level architect.

IT ARCHITECT ROLE

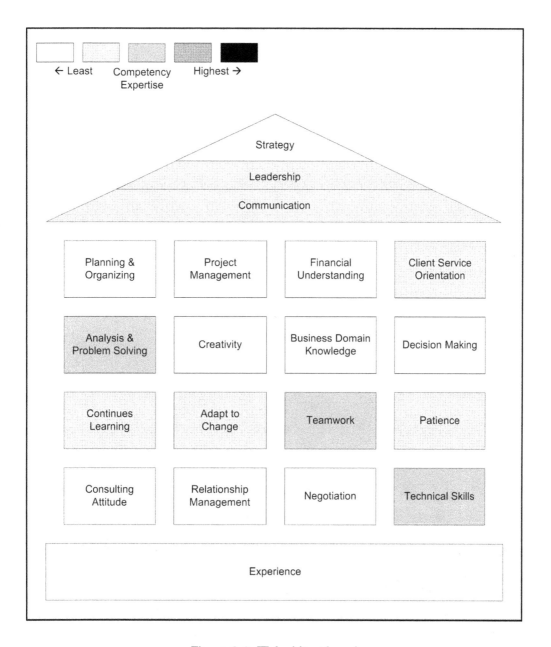

Figure 2-9. IT Architect Level

2.7.2   Senior IT Architect Level

Architects at level 2 have at least 4-7 years of experience in architecting systems and have participated in larger, complex system designs. Architects have developed architecture leadership roles and a deep understanding of designing multiple systems and resolving complex systems problems. Architects have the capability to lead larger initiatives and mentor other IT architects. Architects contribute to the advancement of the architecture practice within organizations. This includes standards, knowledge, training and coaching.

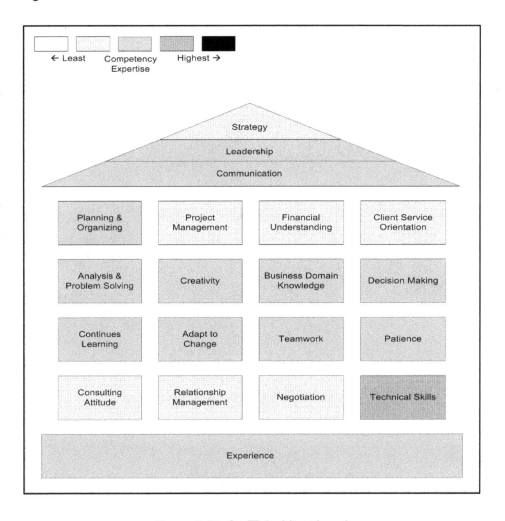

Figure 2-10. Sr. IT Architect Level

2.7.3   Program/Portfolio IT Architect Level

Architects at level 3 have at least 7-10 years of experience in architecting systems and have led multiple, larger complex system designs. Architects at this level are senior architects who have developed an even broader knowledge and are responsible for an entire program or portfolio. Architects have developed strong architecture leadership roles and strong relationships with program and portfolio managers and executives. Architects have a dedicated architecture program or portfolio in which they oversee and manage the architecture direction of an area. Architects are responsible for directing other architects and/or senior architects that are working on a project within their program or portfolio. Architects make a significant contribution to the advancement of the architecture practice within organizations. This includes standards, knowledge, training and coaching.

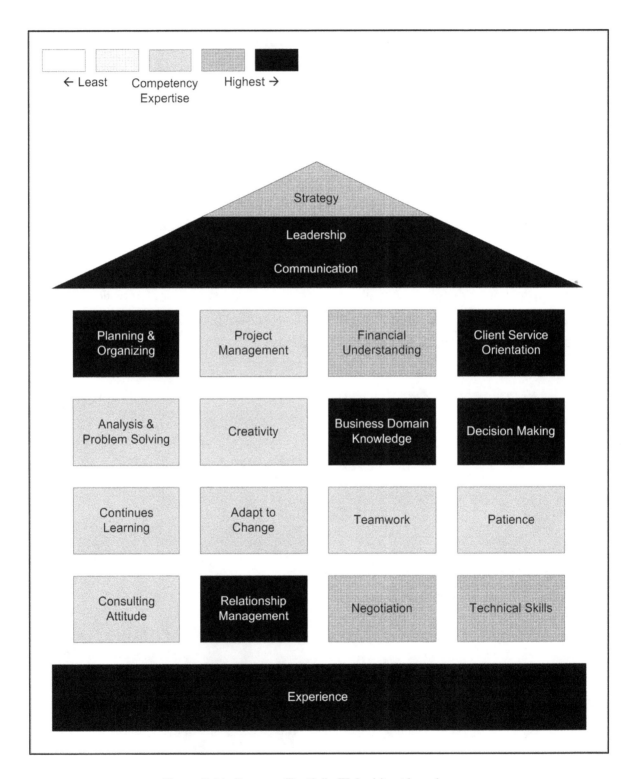

Figure 2-11. Program/Portfolio IT Architect Level

2.7.4   Enterprise/Chief IT Architect Level

Architects at level 4 have at least 10 years experience architecting many systems and have led multiple larger complex system designs. Architects at this level have a very broad scope and oversee the entire architecture of the enterprise. They must have exceptional architecture leadership expertise and have developed strong relationships with senior managers and C level executives. They have a responsibility to set the vision and lead the architectural practice. They are responsible for directing all architects within the organization. They are making a significant contribution to the advancement of the architecture practice within organizations, including training and coaching, standards, and knowledge. They are responsible for the overall architectural governance.

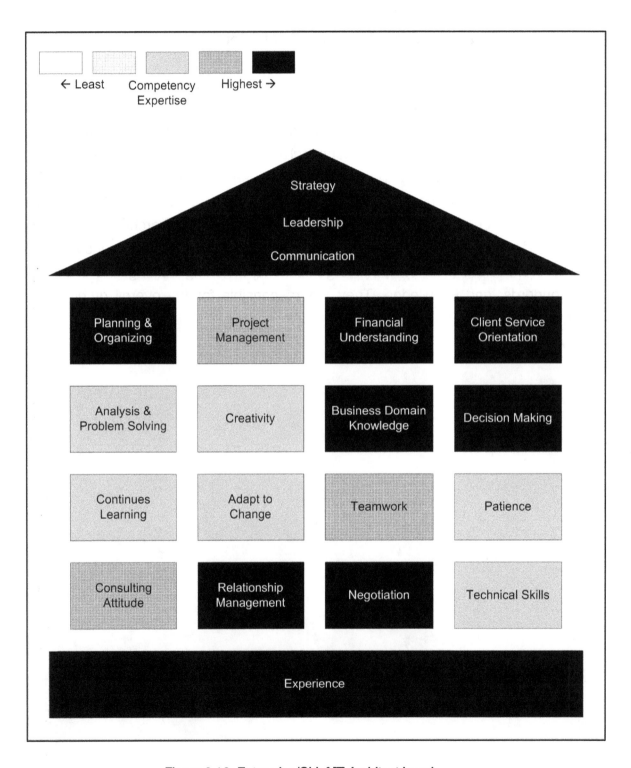

Figure 2-12. Enterprise/Chief IT Architect Level

CHAPTER 3

ARCHITECTURE MANAGEMENT OFFICE (AMO)

The Architecture Management Office (AMO) is a team, a group, or a unit within an organization that establishes, maintains and promotes standards for IT architecture management. AMO's primary objectives are to gain benefits from standardization, build a strong architecture knowledge base, and monitor, govern and promote architecture management policies, frameworks, processes, and methodologies.

This chapter will establish the third part of the foundational knowledge by understanding the AMO practice and how it benefits organizations. This section is broken down as follows:

3.1 AMO Overview

3.2 AMO Components

3.3 AMO Benefits

3.4 AMO Structure

3.5 AMO Funding Model

3.6 Architecture Management Maturity Model

3.1 AMO Overview

One of the most exciting and challenging opportunities is to establish something from scratch. If someone asks the question, How do organizations build an architectural practice such as the AMO?, the answer is that it should be built the same way sky scrapers are built—from a structural and building design perspective. Using this analogy, there are similarities in how organizations can build an architectural practice that will last decades and withstand the rigors of technology and the environment.

The first step is to use a similar approach that traditional building architects use. Survey the site and evaluate the environment by testing to see if it has the elements to build a strong foundation. From an IT perspective, organizations need to ask these questions: What organizational processes and structures do we have? Can we use existing processes and what do we need to build? Do we have management support? How do we build awareness, support and commitment to architecture?

The second step is to establish and build a strong foundation that will be the base for supporting the "skyscraper" or architectural practice. Taking a scientific approach to this analogy, we can identify key ingredients that make up the elements used in building foundations, beams, and columns.

1. The first is concrete (i.e. the Enterprise Architect/Chief Architect) that binds the elements together.

2. The second is stone aggregates (i.e. the architecture resources) which strengthen the foundation by adding chunks of knowledge to the base.

3. The third is water (i.e. ability to change) that has unique and dynamic elements which can activate the concrete's properties to strengthen its position.

4. The fourth and most important is steel (i.e. the CIO); when you add steel

to the mix, you create the structural engineering concept of reinforced concrete. Without the support, commitment and involvement of the CIO, organizations will have a weak architecture foundation.

The third step after the foundation has been established is to start developing education and awareness sessions about the benefits of architecture and how departments can use it. Building awareness is key in getting buy-in from different departments and stakeholders to start utilizing and leveraging AMO services. Establishing architectural principles at the beginning will help set up the practice for a successful start. Such principles may include: data is shared; one patient equals one record; and data must be protected. Establishing architectural processes and methodologies will help guide the organization on how the practice can be engaged and what is required from a documentation and process perspective.

Establishing a good understanding of what is the current state architecture is important, as well as finding the documentation and processes which determines what IT assets organizations currently have. Looking at the target state architecture takes a three to five year business plan and determines the required technology needed to support the plan. Through the development of architecture roadmaps, organizations can build a strategy to take the current state architecture and move it to the target state. Establishing technological and architectural standards will guide the organization in creating synergies through common usage of technology.

The architecture practice will be accountable for the technology life cycle. Organizations have to control the introduction of new technologies and the phasing out of older technologies by leveraging technology roadmaps as a guide. This can help reduce the management of many different systems, tools, and technologies which require a large number of resources to support. Support for projects is a key service of the practice as well as the overall governance model that ensures consistent use and implementation of technology across the enterprise.

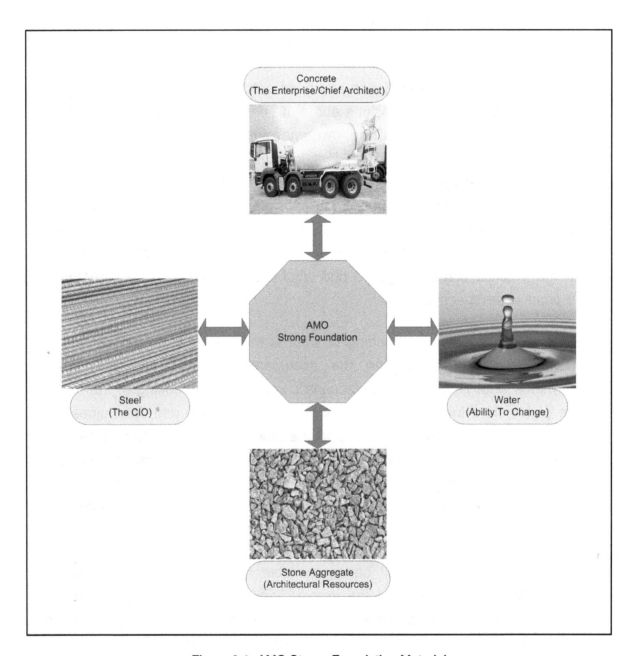

Figure 3-1. AMO Strong Foundation Material

3.2 AMO Components

The AMO practice needs to be established with a strong foundation to give it the support it needs. Architecture governance represented in Figure 3-2 plays a key role in protecting, guiding and monitoring the rules, standards, processes and methodologies, and ensuring that they are being followed through appropriate governance processes. The rest of the AMO twelve components focus on areas that need to be developed and managed. The components level of maturity will depend on how successfully the AMO is being managed and supported.

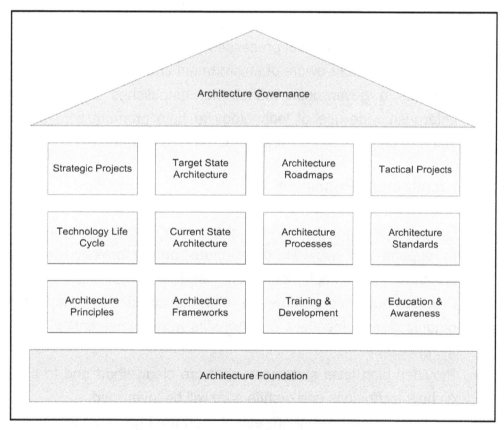

Figure 3-2. AMO Components Framework

3.2.1   Architecture Governance

- Provides guidance and compliance processes on how IT architecture will be used and implemented to assist in projects and technology advancements.
- Establishes an approval and review process to guide the IT architecture and technology environment's growth and future development.
- Provides a check point for alignment of business and IT strategies.
- Focuses on establishing strong architecture resources and promotes excellence and advancements of the concept of architecture.
- Provides management and communication tools for IT architects, and interactions and approval processes to make sure that different levels of IT architects are aware of environment changes.
- Provides a governance model that establishes and enforces an enterprise wide use of technology to help promote consistency for different areas and departments across the enterprise.

3.2.2   Architecture Principles

- General rules and guidelines that are established by the organization to support the way IT architecture and information technology resources will be implemented and used.
- Provides guidance on how the rules can be utilized to help achieve organizational objectives and benefits from implementing and using the principles.
- Provides high level statements that are clear, short and to the point on how technology and architecture will be leveraged.
- Provides principles that are established through direct involvement of businesses, managers, architects, technical resources and executives that have agreed on the name, definitions, rationale and implications of such statements.

3.2.3 Architecture Processes

- A key element of establishing a strong architectural practice through standard processes.
- Provides an execution method for performing a set of tasks in a repeatable and proven way.
- Provides a method for communication, documentation, and identification of the resources required to accomplish the architecture design and deliverables.
- Provides a way toward education and awareness of how architectural techniques are grouped and implemented.
- Provides guidance on development and training of IT architects.
- Improves quality and service delivery through architectural processes that have been designed, built and tested for repeatability and efficiency.
- Provides consistency and business buy-ins using an approved method for providing architectural services. This will limit political bureaucracy and help increase AMO credibility for establishing and governing of processes.

3.2.4 Architecture Standards

- A formal statement that has been approved and acts as the authoritative De facto decision recommendation, selection or acknowledgement of a particular decision, idea or topic.
- Architecture standards have been studied, thought out, and tested to come up with the best decision alternative to be used for future similar decisions in order to improve the quality and speed of decision making.
- Provides an efficient way to handle decision making by referring to the architecture standard as the approved approach for doing things.

- A set of rules that facilitates consistency in selection, designing, and implementing architecture decisions, documentation and designs.

3.2.5 Architecture Frameworks

- A framework documents independent components and provides a reference for the relationship between components.
- Provides a simplified view of how information is organized and categorized to help increase the communication channel hence improving the level of understanding of architectural artifacts.
- Provides guidance for reviewing and analyzing architectural documentation, concepts, and methodologies.
- Provides a view of how architectural artifacts and designs can be shared and communicated between architects, technical resources and other stakeholders.
- Provides an abstraction layer to hide the complexity of designing systems, and establishes the foundational model to be used.

3.2.6 Current State Architecture

- Provides a high level view of existing architecture, systems, technologies, integration, and interfaces.
- Provides a document for existing processes that includes both business and technology domains.
- Provides a view of system dependencies and how they are used by business units.
- Provides a view of how systems are integrated with internal and external systems and what technologies are used for integration and how they can be traced for dependency analysis.
- Provides a view for management of existing assets to determine how they can be utilized and when they need to be changed and phased

out. This improves decision making as it facilitates understanding of what exists today.

- Provides an efficient way to do impact assessment of technology changes and promotes how these assets can be used to help reduce redundant application.

- Provides a mechanism to use for educating new architects as well as sharing knowledge with business users to help them appreciate the value of architecture.

3.2.7   Target State Architecture

- Provides the organization's vision of how information technology capabilities will be in the next five years, using architecture as the tool to guide this process.

- Provides the business and technology alignment, and maps how existing IT assets will look in five years to support business and IT strategies.

- Provides the ability for business and IT to work together and plan out how IT infrastructure and systems will provide the business services in the most efficient way, while making the best use of assets and resources.

- Provides a tool to help establish a list of architecture projects and initiatives that will support the needs of the business.

- Provides a vision for architects to work toward as they implement tactical and strategic projects.

- Acts as guidance toward where the organization is heading as it relates to their IT capabilities.

3.2.8 Architecture Roadmaps

- Provides guidance on how the current state architecture will move toward the target state architecture over the next five years of architecture planning.

- Provides a list of gaps between the current and target state architecture and shows how the gaps will be addressed by highlighting the incremental changes required to close them using initiatives and projects.

- Provides a view for understanding how the business needs will be impacted by the changes required and the corresponding timeframe.

- Provides a pictorial view that demonstrates how the architecture vision will be moving from current to target state.

- Provides a source for understanding the efforts, resources, and dependencies required during the architecture transition phase between current and target state.

3.2.9 Technology Lifecycle Management

- Technology continues to evolve and change at a high rate that makes it necessary to implement an appropriate technology lifecycle management process to govern the way organizations introduce and phase out technology.

- Balancing between project support and technology changes requires a good governance model that ensures consistent use and implementation of technology across the enterprise in the most efficient and cost effective manner.

- Figure 3.3 illustrates how organizations can implement six phases for technology deployment.

- The technology assessment phase is established to identify business objectives and how technology will be used to satisfy the objectives.

- The IT infrastructure phase determines the infrastructure needs and how it will be selected, purchased and implemented.
- The IT integration phase determines how the different technologies will be integrated and deployed.
- The IT support phase determines the warranty, maintenance, SLA, system administration and monitoring needs.
- The technology refresh cycle phase includes decisions to upgrade or replace with newer technologies. The refresh activities have to be done in a timely, organized and scheduled manner to reduce the risk and impact to the organization.
- The technology disposition phase determines assets that have to be disposed with and taken out of the environment in the most cost effective and efficient way.

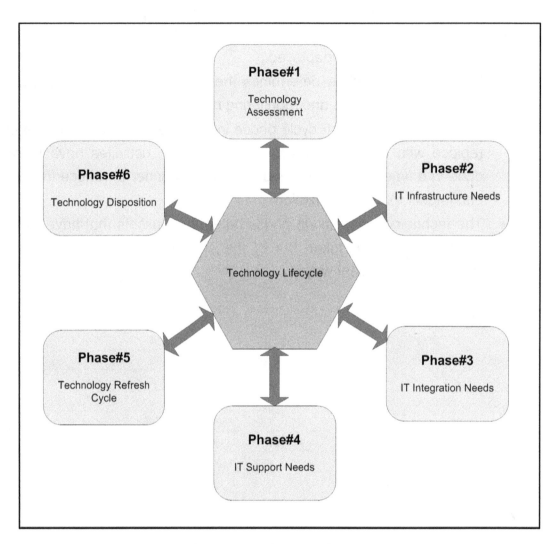

Figure 3.3 Technology Lifecycle

3.2.10   Tactical Projects

- Tactical projects require immediate to short term solutions and cannot wait for the strategic architecture direction.
- Tactical projects are typically in-year projects that may require an architecture exception if they do not meet the architecture standard but are required for immediate business needs.
- Business units that are responsible for the tactical projects are typically required to revisit the technology decision and make the appropriate investments to bring the chosen technology or decision to standard compliance.

3.2.11   Strategic Projects

- Strategic projects are designed to address the business strategic direction that tends to span multiple years and usually requires a bigger capital and resources investment.
- Strategic projects are usually more complex and very well funded. Architects use this project opportunity to move the organization closer to the target state architecture—if planned properly.

3.2.12   Training & Development

- Training and development is a critical factor in the success of the architecture practice. Individuals need to be aware of the processes and procedures that are implemented through appropriate training.
- Career development plans for architects will increase their knowledge and strengthen the architects' abilities.
- Training is an integral part of the life of an architect as it is required to stay abreast of new technologies and design patterns.

3.2.13   Education & Awareness

- Education and awareness provides a means of communication to the people within the AMO office as well as external partners and business units that utilize AMO services.
- The more people are educated about what the AMO does, the better the interaction and understanding of how to use, promote and engage the architectural practice.

3.3 AMO Benefits

AMO benefits can include but are not limited to an AMO unit that has the properties of a centre of excellence for providing IT architecture services and expertise—an efficient and effective resource sharing model that has architecture processes, standards, portfolio support, improved project success—and saves money. AMO is a place that provides guidance and mentoring for IT architects, a place architects can call home, a place for building a strong team atmosphere and a sense of belonging. It is a place for sharing and providing knowledge, self evaluation, performance metrics, and a place which provides IT architect career planning services.

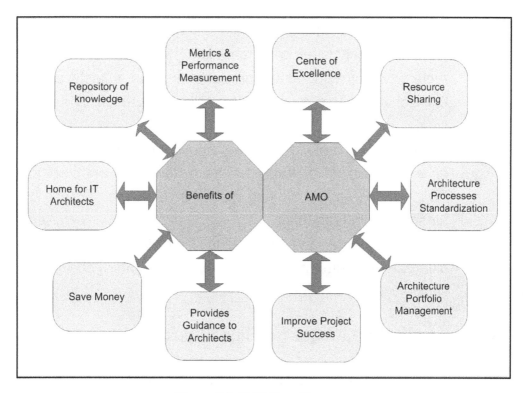

Figure 3.4 AMO Benefits

3.3.1 Centre of Excellence

- AMO is a centre of excellence for architecture where the knowledge, expertise, resources and direction are managed by the AMO office.
- AMO architecture team members who work on projects bring knowledge, lessons learned, and improvement opportunities back to the AMO office to find ways to optimize existing architecture processes.
- AMO creates mentoring relationships between architects. They share domain knowledge and learn technical expertise from each other.

3.3.2 Resource Sharing

- AMO provides a central way to share architecture resources such as processes, techniques and architects.
- Architects are assigned to a project or multiple projects, depending on the workload. This results in maximum utilization of the architects' time.
- Architects are senior resources, and some business units may not have the demand or funds to hire a dedicated architect to support their area. Resource sharing makes architecture services affordable for smaller departments.
- Resource sharing gives architects the ability to provide services to different departments. It also expands their business domain knowledge and expertise.

3.3.3 Architecture Processes Standardization

- AMO provides the means to standardize architecture practices and techniques so all architects are aware of the processes that are used consistently on projects.
- AMO standardization delivers a fast, efficient and effective way to leverage architecture services regardless of who the assigned

architect resource is. It provides and follows a consistent and well understood process.

- AMO standardization creates a way to communicate with different business units in a consistent manner that they can understand. AMO engagement processes and the overall service delivery should be consistent.
- AMO standardization provides a standard tools platform to allow architecture deliverables to be documented, shared and communicated consistently.
- AMO standardization leverages industry standards in the use of methodologies and processes.

3.3.4   Architecture Portfolio Management

- AMO facilitates the assignment and management of an architecture portfolio for a business unit that has a portfolio of projects that require architecture involvement.
- Architecture portfolio management streamlines the list of projects and their dependencies by working with business unit managers, executives, and the project management office.
- Architecture portfolio management tends to be a multiyear assignment for dedicated portfolio architects who manage the architecture lifecycle and projects within that portfolio.
- Architecture portfolio management builds strong relationships and close visibility with the business unit. It provides a deeper understanding of the type of business activities executed and the IT support required.

3.3.5   Improves Project Success

- AMO establishes a strong architecture presence with well organized and established processes. Architects can provide an architecture service that supports a well thought out system design. Architects' identification of project and technical risks and their associated mitigation strategies improves the project success rate and results in a better product.

- AMO helps increase the project success rate by providing architects with the knowledge, tools and techniques to answer and solve some of common issues and problems which arise in projects.

3.3.6   Provides Guidance to Architects

- AMO acts as an overarching body that provides guidance and support for IT architects.
- AMO provides support, mentoring and career development opportunities for IT architects.
- AMO establishes standard procedures and processes for IT architects to help them execute projects more effectively.
- AMO guidance includes but is not limited to education, training, mentoring, coaching, and monthly group meetings.

3.3.7   Save Money

- AMO saves money through the effective utilization of IT architects and architecture resources such as documentation, processes and standards.
- AMO provides the ability to smaller business units to receive architecture services without having to spend a lot of money to hire a dedicated architect.
- AMO saves money by helping projects use existing knowledge, best practices and lessons learned to avoid costly mistakes.
- AMO saves money through effective resource management, by reducing project failures and providing support for strategic projects that can yield substantial value to the organization.

3.3.8 Home for IT Architects

- AMO creates for architects a sense of belonging to a group of individuals that are dedicated to the IT architecture profession.
- AMO supports architects by providing a sense of home when they are not working on projects. Architects can use the down time to work on AMO internal initiatives until they get reassigned to project work.
- AMO provides the opportunity to share knowledge and document best practices by attending AMO meetings to help strengthen the bond between architects.

3.3.9 Repository for Knowledge

- AMO acts as a source where one collects and shares knowledge from project experiences, seminars, training and conferences.
- AMO facilitates the architect's involvement in creating templates, processes and standards documents that can be shared and accessed by other architects in the group.
- AMO takes charge of document management, updates and distributes information to all architects.
- AMO collects project knowledge that can be further fine-tuned in additional projects where new patterns and design options can be tested.
- AMO collects and summarizes lessons learned, best practices and architecture risks that can be analyzed, documented and communicated to architects.

3.3.10   Metrics & Performance Measurement

- AMO provides metrics and performance measurement results on how the architects and the AMO as a practice are performing. The measurements can be used as a score card to help find improvement opportunities.
- AMO provides measurement of how project requests are being handled and how their staffing needs are meeting business unit demands.
- AMO reviews project architecture reports and conducts formal evaluations of architects to provide feedback for career advancements.

3.4 AMO Structure

AMO structure can vary depending on how established the organization's architectural practice is. Organizations can fall into five categories that relate to architecture structure. First category resembles an organization that has no AMO practice and no IT architects in their IT department, and they rely on technical people. Second category resembles an organization that has no AMO practice but has a single IT architect typically reporting to an IT Manager. Third category resembles an organization that has no AMO practice but has a few IT architects, typically reporting to different IT managers in different teams and supporting different business units. Fourth category resembles an organization that has an AMO with a few too many IT architects. These architects are centrally structured and report to the AMO Manager and are deployed to different projects to provide architecture services to the enterprise. Fifth category resembles an organization that has a very well established AMO practice with a large pool of IT architects with varied experiences and levels, supporting departments, large portfolios and the enterprise.

Architecture Structure Category Summary:
1. No AMO + No IT Architects
2. No AMO + Single IT Architect
3. No AMO + Few IT Architects
4. AMO + A few too many IT architects
5. AMO + Many IT architects

3.4.1   Architecture Structure Category #1

Architecture structure's first category represents an organization that has no AMO practice and no IT architects in their IT department. They rely solely on technical people. If the organization is a very small company with a few IT staff supporting basic infrastructure components and applications, then it is acceptable not to have an IT architect. However, if this is a medium to large organization then it may not be acceptable. The missed opportunities of architectural benefits certainly outweigh the cost associated with having at least one or a few IT architects and moving towards category #2 or #3 structure.

<u>Advantages:</u>
- None.

<u>Disadvantages:</u>
- Missed opportunity to leverage architectural benefits.

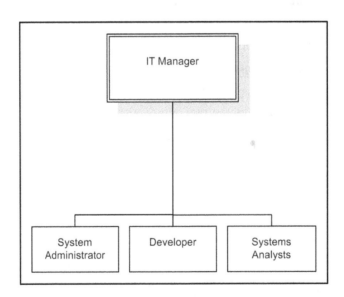

Figure 3.5 Architecture Structure Category #1

3.4.2   Architecture Structure Category #2

Architecture structure's second category represents an organization that has no AMO practice but has a single IT architect typically reporting to an IT Manager.

<u>Advantages:</u>
- Easy to implement. One architect reports to the IT manager and works with the technical team to set architecture guidance.
- Dedicated IT architect for the team to help understand business unit needs and systems.

<u>Disadvantages:</u>
- If the IT architect is not fully utilized on projects, it may result in underutilization where the architect could be supporting other teams with a centralized AMO model.

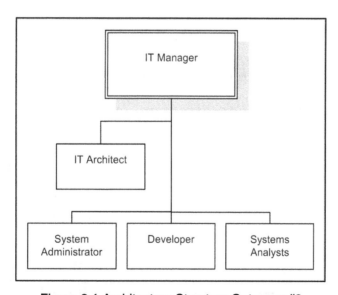

Figure 3.6 Architecture Structure Category #2

3.4.3   Architecture Structure Category #3

Architecture structure's third category represents an organization that has no AMO practice but has a few IT architects typically reporting to different IT managers in different teams and supporting different business units.

Advantages:

- Easy to implement. Each architect reports to the IT manager and works with the technical team to set architecture guidance.
- Flexibility is given to the IT managers to hire their own dedicated IT architect.
- Architecture benefits are realized but are localized to the team or business unit.

Disadvantages:

- Requires good coordination between IT architects. Conflicts may arise when priorities for each of the architect's are set by different manager.
- Knowledge sharing may be impacted if IT architects are not communicating due to team and project separation.
- Standards processes, methodologies and frameworks will be harder to implement in a decentralized structure.

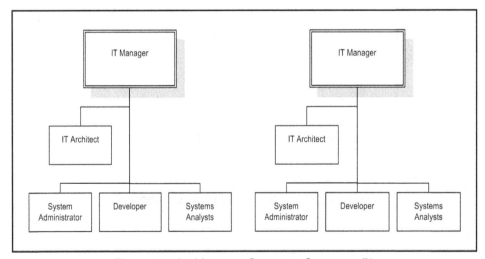

Figure 3.7 Architecture Structure Category #3

3.4.4   Architecture Structure Category #4

Architecture structure's fourth category represents an organization that has an AMO with a few too many IT architects. Architects are centrally structured and report to the AMO Manager and are deployed to different projects to provide architecture services to the enterprise.

Advantages:

- A centrally shared model that can leverage architecture resources in an efficient and effective way.
- Refer to section 3.3 for a list of AMO benefits.

Disadvantages:

- Requires upfront commitment and support of the organization to establish the AMO practice and cover the operational costs. However, the benefits of the architecture practice will outweigh the costs once benefits are fully realized.

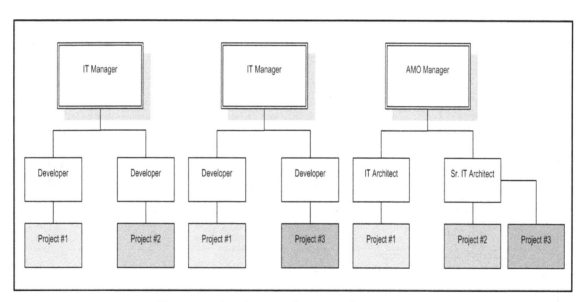

Figure 3.8 Architecture Structure Category #4

3.4.5 Architecture Structure Category #5

Architecture structure's fifth category represents an organization that has a very well established AMO practice with a large pool of IT architects, with varied experiences and levels, supporting departments, large portfolios and the support of the whole enterprise.

Advantages:
- A centrally shared model that can leverage architecture resources in an efficient and effective way.
- Refer to section 3.3 for a list of AMO benefits.

Disadvantages:
- Requires significant investment and long term commitment to establish a very large architecture practice. However, the benefits of the architecture practice will outweigh the costs once benefits are fully realized.

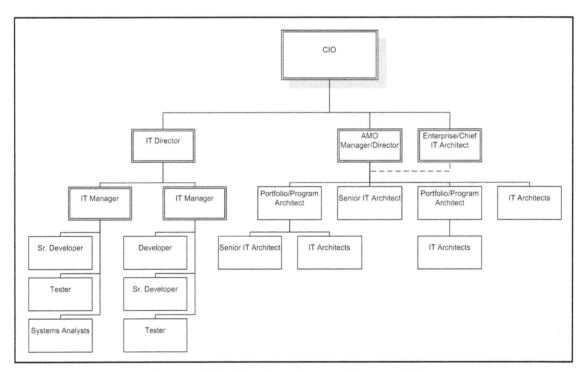

Figure 3.9 Architecture Structure Category #5

3.5 AMO Funding Model

The AMO funding model varies, depending on the organizational structure, culture and financial models that are in place. The existing financial process may influence how an organization implements the AMO practice. A centralized vs. decentralized organization structure, resources sharing, charge back models and culture will affect how the AMO is funded. Nevertheless, there are two models that can be used: the fully funded central model and the partially funded consultancy model.

3.5.1   Fully Funded Central Model

The fully funded central model has financial investment and the commitment of the organization to fund the AMO operations. This includes things such as AMO management and IT architect salaries, facilities, equipment, training, and operational expenses.

Advantages
- The AMO has the full financial investment of the organization. This creates more stability.
- Less financial and management overhead since salaries, expenses, and operational costs are covered by the organization. This still requires using existing finances and management processes, but the pressure to maintain a constant revenue source to cover the operational and salary costs for IT architects is reduced.

Disadvantages
- The expansion of the AMO practice may be limited to the yearly budgetary and demand forecast for increasing headcount. This results in a slower growth cycle.
- Possible reduction in expanding the IT architect services and head count during high demands. This will have to be addressed during the yearly budget cycle process.

- Distribution of IT architecture services to departments may be challenging during busy times—since departments contribute a percentage of the support cost to fund the AMO practice.

3.5.2 Partially Funded Consultancy Model

The partially funded consultancy model has partial investment to cover the cost for the core team. This typically includes the AMO management team salary and some of the operational expenses such as facilities and equipments. IT architects are internally billable to departments requiring architecture services. The revenue generated by the internal consultancy model will be used to cover the salaries for the IT architects and other associated expenses. This model requires more creative management and good financial management to maintain the constant source of revenue necessary to maintain and grow the AMO practice.

Advantages
- The ability to grow the team very quickly based on the demand for services.
- The AMO management team and IT architects have a strong interest to promote, manage and increase the services offered to departments.
- Departments are clients for the IT architecture team, and a services mentality and customer relationship play a key role in building strong, long term partnerships with departments.

Disadvantages
- When demand decreases for IT architecture services so will the revenue to maintain the AMO practice, resulting in possible downsizing or redeployment of members to other teams.
- More financial and management overhead for internal billing and revenue forecast analysis.

3.6 Architecture Management Maturity Model

The architecture management maturity model leverages the Capability Maturity Model (CMM) that was developed by the Software Engineering Institute at Carnegie Mellon University (www.sei.cmu.edu). The CMM has been widely used and adapted to other areas to include Enterprise Architecture, Project Management, and Risk Management. The architecture management maturity model can assist organizations to determine how well their architecture management practices are performing and the practices' level of maturity. This can assist in establishing development and growth opportunities to support, measure and continually improve the architecture practice.

The architecture management maturity model has five maturity levels:

- *Level 1 = Initial*
    - o Very little or no focus on architecture management.

- *Level 2 = Repeatable*
    - o Architecture management activities are established with some individually repeatable activities.

- *Level 3 = Defined*
    - o Architecture management activities are well defined and used consistently.

- *Level 4 = Managed*
    - o Architecture management activities are measured and controlled.

- *Level 5 = Optimizing*
    - o Architecture management activities are under continuous improvement efforts.

There are five architecture management factors that are evaluated to determine the level of maturity.

- *Administration*
  - Management structure, teams, roles, and responsibilities.

- *Processes*
  - Processes, standards, principles, and documentation.

- *Communication*
  - Strategies, methods and approaches for architecture communication.

- *Involvement*
  - Sr. Management, departments, and AMO involvement and awareness.

- *Growth*
  - Financial growth, services expansion, headcount growth, IT architect career development, and AMO stability.

3.6.1   Maturity Level I - Initial

The initial level of maturity has very little or no focus on architecture management. Organizations at this level demonstrate the following statements about the architecture management factors:

- *Administration*
  - Informal architecture management structure.
  - A few architects are localized and part of different IT teams.

- o Roles and responsibilities may be different between localized architects.
- *Processes*
  - o Limited processes with ad hoc and informal usage.
  - o Limited to no standards or principles.
  - o Partial documentation may exist but is scattered and not consistent.
- *Communication*
  - o Very little communication over the architecture practice.
  - o Limited ad hoc communication between localized architects from different teams.
- *Involvement*
  - o No Sr. Management or department involvement.
  - o Limited organization awareness of architecture.
  - o Some localized involvement by managers responsible for the architects on their team.
- *Growth*
  - o Limited to no growth in financial, services and architect headcount.
  - o A few localized architects working for different teams with limited career development required to grow to higher architect levels.

3.6.2   Maturity Level 2 - Repeatable

The repeatable level of maturity has architecture management activities that are partially established with some individually repeatable activities. Organizations at this level demonstrate the following statements about the architecture management factors:

- *Administration*
  - o Formal but small AMO structure with clear roles and responsibilities.
  - o A few architects with a matrix reporting structure to the AMO providing localized architecture support to IT teams.
- *Processes*
  - o Processes, standards and principles are documented and established at the project level.
  - o Documentation templates have been developed and are being used.
  - o Documentation repositories have been established but not completed.
- *Communication*
  - o AMO practice has a formal website. Communication strategies and channels are developed, and practice activities are being communicated.
  - o Communications between architect and the AMO is clearly defined and used.
- *Involvement*
  - o Sr. Management and departments are aware of AMO activities and efforts.
  - o AMO is involved with different departments and units to increase architecture awareness.

- *Growth*
  - o Limited financial, services and architect headcount growth. More analysis and architecture services forecasting will need to be established to secure additional funds and growth opportunities.
  - o Career development plans, performance reviews and a path toward higher architect levels have been established.

3.6.3   Maturity Level 3 - Defined

The defined level of maturity has architecture management activities that are well defined and used consistently. Organizations at this level demonstrate the following statements about the architecture management factors:

- *Administration*
  - o AMO is well defined, staffed, and established.
  - o Architects have a direct reporting structure to the AMO and provide architecture services and support to the enterprise.
- *Processes*
  - o Processes, standards and principles are well documented, communicated and used consistently.
  - o Documentation templates and repositories are established and complete.
  - o Architecture governance, frameworks, models are adopted and used.
- *Communication*
  - o AMO practice has a well established online presence, utilizing websites, wikis and portals for effective and efficient communication.
  - o Communication strategies and channels are well established and practice activities are being communicated and accepted by the general audience.

- o Active communications and participation between architects, the AMO , IT teams, and business departments.
- *Involvement*
  - o Sr. Management and departments are supporting AMO activities and efforts.
  - o AMO is involved with the organization's strategic planning activities to coordinate and plan architecture activities.
- *Growth*
  - o Sr. Management has financial and operational commitment to grow architecture services and increase the architects' staffing needs.
  - o Clear career development plans, training needs, and performance review processes are well established and used.

3.6.4   Maturity Level 4 - Managed

The managed level of maturity has architecture management activities that are well defined, measured and controlled. Organizations at this level demonstrate the following statements about the architecture management factors:

- *Administration*
  - o AMO financial performance and staff utilization are being measured.
  - o AMO architecture services are being measured for quality, and client satisfaction surveys are being conducted.
- *Processes*
  - o Processes, standards and principles are part of the organization's culture, and quality measurements are being captured.
  - o Architecture documentation and repositories are being reviewed and analyzed for quality.
  - o Control measures have been implemented through architecture review and approval committees.

- *Communication*
  - AMO practice has a well established online presence, utilizing websites, wikis, portals, blogs and collaboration tools.
  - Communication strategies and channels are measured for quality and include feedback mechanisms to rate communication effectiveness.
- *Involvement*
  - Sr. Management and departments are involved in important AMO activities, efforts and decisions.
  - AMO is involved and has some influence over the organization's strategic planning activities to coordinate and plan architecture activities.
  - AMO's knowledge and expertise is gaining internal and external visibility by participating in architecture groups, conferences, and standards bodies.
- *Growth*
  - AMO service offers expansion, and IT architects staff headcount growth is being measured.
  - IT architect training objectives, career and level growth are measured.

3.6.5   Maturity Level 5 - Optimizing

The optimizing level of maturity has architecture management activities that are undergoing continuous improvement efforts. Organizations at this level demonstrate the following statements about the architecture management factors:

- *Administration*
    - AMO financial performance and staff utilization are being measured and optimized to reduce operational expenses and increase staff utilization.
    - AMO architecture services are being measured for quality, and optimization of performance, and improved to increase client satisfaction results.
- *Processes*
    - Processes, standards and principles are measured and evaluated for improvement.
    - Architecture documentation and repositories are measured and reviewed for optimization opportunities.
    - AMO contributes knowledge and expertise to industry standards development.
- *Communication*
    - AMO practice has a well established online presence, utilizing websites, wikis, portals, blogs and collaboration tools.
    - Communication strategies and channels are measured for quality and are optimized for effectiveness.
- *Involvement*
    - AMO is very involved and has influence over the organization's strategic planning activities to plan and fund strategic architecture activities.
    - AMO is recognized internally and externally as major contributors to knowledge of architecture and standards bodies.
- *Growth*
    - AMO services and IT architects headcount is being measured and optimized to offer more services with controlled staff increases.
    - IT architect training objectives, career and level growth is measured and optimized to have staff at different levels well trained and motivated.

ARCHITECTURE MANAGEMENT OFFICE (AMO)

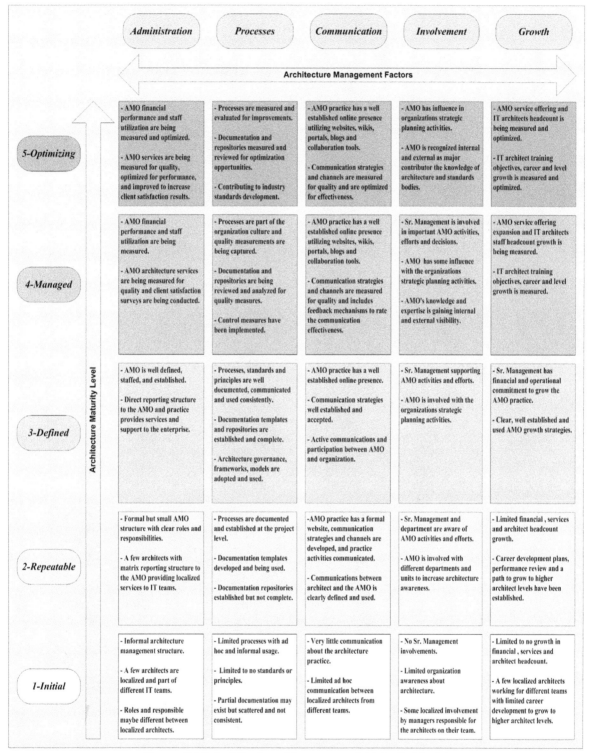

Figure 3.10 Architecture Management Maturity Model

SECTION II

ARCHITECTURE MANAGEMENT PROCESSES

Chapter 4

- Architecture Management Life Cycle

Chapter 5

- Project Management Integration

CHAPTER 4

ARCHITECTURE MANAGEMENT LIFE CYCLE

Architecture management life cycle describes the different stages that IT architecture management goes through from its inception to completion. It also defines the processes and how they are managed and controlled between the different stages. It is a cycle where one process output feeds the process input, and process dependencies may cause processes to get invoked again to capture the updates.

This chapter will establish the core processes that are required to effectively manage the IT architecture components of a project. This section is broken down as follows:

4.1 Architecture Management Life Cycle Overview

4.2 Architecture Engagement Processes

4.3 Architecture Analysis Processes

4.4 Architecture Design Processes

4.5 Architecture Implementation Processes

4.6 Architecture Realization Processes

4.1   Architecture Management Life Cycle Overview

Architecture management life cycle (AMLC) defines a set of five major processes that IT architecture management goes through from its initial engagement to architecture realization. The five architecture management stages are engagement, analysis, design, implementation and realization. Architecture documentation represents an important part of the life cycle as it includes a living document of the design components of the system, software or application. The last stage of the life cycle is referenced as architecture realization. It is the essence that takes the architecture blueprints and makes it real through a working system that has achieved the architected design. Using an example from building architecture, architects always must have recent and up-to-date architecture blueprints that include the latest modification or addition. They need blueprints in order to be sure they fully understand the structure of the building before recommending any changes. IT architecture needs to use the same model and have a repository of the latest architecture artifacts to be utilized and maintained.

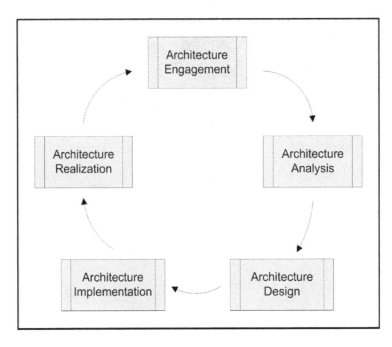

Figure 4-1. Architecture Management Life Cycle Model

4.1.1   Architecture Engagement Overview

Architecture engagement is the first phase of the architecture management processes to determine the engagement, assessment and scoping of the IT architecture work required. This phase helps establish the guidelines and methods in which the architecture work will be undertaken for a particular project. An estimation of the level of involvement can also be highlighted in the engagement and assessment document.

4.1.2   Architecture Analysis Overview

Architecture analysis is the second phase of the architecture management processes to determine the scope of the problem architects are trying to solve. Architects use architecture techniques and acquired knowledge to assist them in the analysis. This will help fine tune the level of effort and estimation numbers that were established during the engagement phase. The analysis phase tends to be a fact finding and documentation journey. Architects collect as much knowledge as they can in the areas being investigated to give them the best methods to tackle problems and design challenges, using architecture patterns and techniques. A considerable amount of time is spent during this phase to grasp all the different angles of looking at the problem at hand.

4.1.3   Architecture Design Overview

Architecture design is the third phase of the architecture management processes to determine the design options and architecture patterns that will be used. The analysis conducted in the second phase will be used as input into the design process. In this phase, architects utilize their experience in how similar problems were solved in the past and how design and architecture will meet the business requirements in the most efficient and effective way. A considerable amount of time is spent during this phase to grasp all the different design options and alternatives. It is much easier to detect design errors at this level before a single line of code is written or any system configuration is done. If the design is done exceptionally well, the implementation phase will go smoothly, and support efforts and maintenance costs for the system will be reduced.

4.1.4   Architecture Implementation Overview

Architecture implementation is the fourth phase of the architecture management processes. Architects will take the architecture blueprint and work with different teams such as developers, testers, infrastructure personnel, system administrators, and DBAs and guide them through the implementation of the design. IT architects play a key role in mentoring and monitoring development in conjunction with the project manager. Architects guide the technical components and ensure that the project progression is on track. Any design issues or problems that might surface during the implementation phase should be brought to the architects' attention to deal with and solve.

4.1.5   Architecture Realization Overview

Architecture realization is the fifth and last phase of the of the architecture management processes. Architects finalize any documentation for the system and educate support teams on the implemented design. Architects submit all documentation to the architecture repository and provide a final report to the AMO. The architecture documentation and blueprints of the system need to be living documents. Any changes to the system after the project is completed need to be noted. Project status and feedback reports need to be communicated to bigger architecture practice initiatives such as enterprise architecture programs.

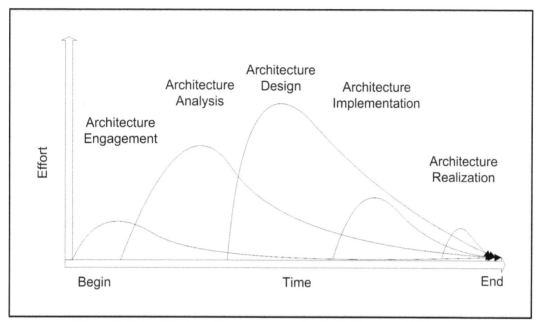

Figure 4-2. Architecture Management Life Cycle Time and Effort Scale

Figure 4-2 illustrates the five stages of AMLC and how they overlap in time. The effort scale indicator represents how much time is relative to the other stages within the AMLC model. Architects spend a great deal of time in the analysis and design phases to makes sure that they have all the information they need to make design decisions. Good analysis leads to a wealth of information that architects can use to determine the architecture design options. The implementation phase could be a lengthy duration of time, but the architects' involvement tends to last that duration to help monitor and guide the building and implementation process.

4.2 Architecture Engagement Processes

Architecture engagement is the first phase of the architecture management processes to determine the engagement, assessment and scoping of the IT architecture work required. This phase helps establish the guidelines and methods in which architecture work will be undertaken for a particular project. A detailed estimation of the level of involvement can also be highlighted in the engagement and assessment document. Figure 4-3 illustrates a high level overview of the processes involved in the engagement phase, including its associated inputs, methods & strategies, and outputs. The first process is 4.2.1 Establish Architecture Engagement and the second process is 4.2.2 Conduct Architecture Assessment.

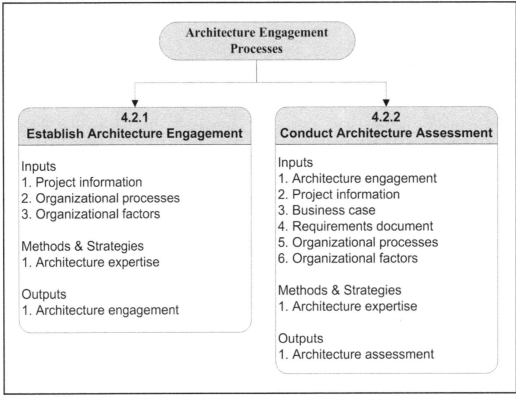

Figure 4-3. Architecture Engagement Processes Overview

Figure 4-4 illustrates the interaction diagram for the architecture engagement processes. Organization specific processes contribute to the engagement processes by providing inputs such as project information, business cases, requirements, organizational processes and factors.

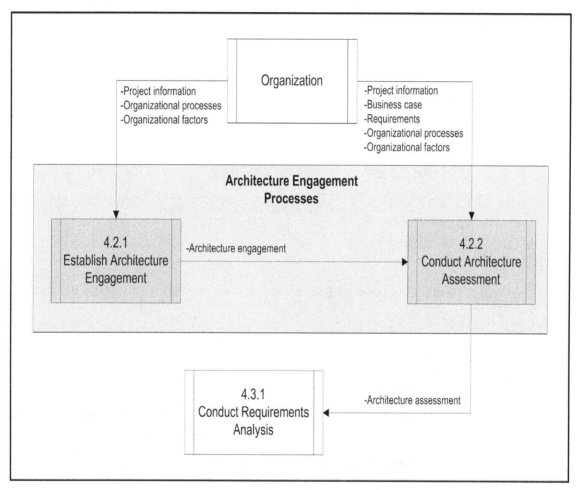

Figure 4-4. Architecture Engagement Interaction Diagram

4.2.1 Establish Architecture Engagement

The establish architecture engagement is a process for evaluating the type of architecture services being requested. It acts as a formal document that highlights the AMO understanding of the IT architecture services requested by the departments or units. The engagement document includes but is not limited to who is requesting the architecture work, the business unit responsible for the project, the charge back model for the services, the architect that will be assigned to the project, a brief description of the project, the length and scope of the project, and the date when the architecture service is required.

Inputs	Methods & Strategies	Outputs
1. Project information 2. Organizational processes 3. Organizational factors	1. Architecture expertise	1. Architecture engagement

Figure 4-5. Establish Architecture Engagement: Inputs, Methods & Strategies, and Outputs

Establish Architecture Engagement: Inputs

1. Project information includes but is not limited to:

   o The project charter is a great resource that will give the architect most of the information required to complete the architecture engagement document. If a project charter does not exist, any documentation describing the project can be used.

   o Verbal descriptions and information by the requesting department can be used to attain some of the required information. This can then be verified and signed by both the AMO and the department requesting the architecture services.

2. Organizational processes include but are not limited to:

   o Company specific processes that include how departments request services from each other.

   o Company specific processes that determine how charge backs and internal funding transfer processes operate between departments.

3. Organizational factors include but are not limited to:

   o Organizational structure and how it may affect project ownership, funding, and matrix reporting structure.

   o Organizational culture and how it may affect changes, and adoption of new architecture processes.

Establish Architecture Engagement: Methods & Strategies

1. Architecture expertise includes but is not limited to:

   o The architect and AMO expertise in building strong relationships with departments to understand their business needs and direction.

   o Leverage the architect's domain expertise for project assignments by matching the architect skills and project needs.

   o The AMO and architects' familiarity with which systems and technologies support which department.

Establish Architecture Engagement: Outputs

1. Architecture engagement document includes but is not limited to:

   o A formal document capturing the project specific information and the type, effort and scope of the architecture engagement.

   o A document that can be used as the AMO service contract with the requesting department.

o A document that can be used as input for metrics to summarize AMO service offers, demand analysis, and architect utilization for monthly, quarterly or yearly reporting.

4.2.2 Conduct Architecture Assessment

Conduct architecture assessment is a process that establishes the basic architecture understanding of the project requirements: the architecture engagement document, project requirement document, and project information documents (such as the charter document). The business case and organizational processes will help the architect achieve a high level understanding of the architecture requirements. The assessment document will focus on the high level scope of the project, the architecture requirements, what systems are impacted, and what are the integration needs. This will help determine the high level of work effort required for conducting the architecture services.

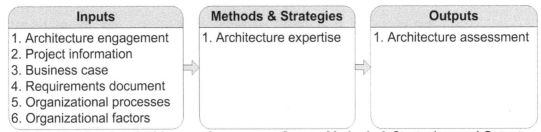

Inputs	Methods & Strategies	Outputs
1. Architecture engagement 2. Project information 3. Business case 4. Requirements document 5. Organizational processes 6. Organizational factors	1. Architecture expertise	1. Architecture assessment

Figure 4-6. Conduct Architecture Assessment: Inputs, Methods & Strategies, and Outputs

Conduct Architecture Assessment: Inputs

1. Architecture engagement document includes but is not limited to:

   o The architecture engagement document that was produced from process 4.2.1 Establish Architecture Engagement.

2. Project information includes but is not limited to:

   o The project charter can be used as a great source for giving the architect the project purpose, funding, stakeholders and the objective of the project. If a project charter does not exist, any documentation describing the project can be used.

- o Communication with initial project members to determine the areas being impacted by the project and any high level architecture considerations that need to be accounted for.

3. Business case includes but not is limited to:

- o Provides the architect with information to help quantify the ROI and builds a strong base for designing the architecture components based on the business drivers. For example, if one of the drivers is speed to market, then the system must be flexible to allow for quick speed to market changes and customization of the system.

4. Requirements document includes but is not limited to:

- o Provides the architect with the means to map out how the architecture will satisfy such requirements.

- o Input to the architecture requirement to determine the scope and features that need to be assessed.

5. Organizational processes include but are not limited to:

- o Company specific processes that highlight the scope and communication methods for assessment results.

6. Organizational factors includes but are not:

- o Organizational structure and culture that may affect assessment reporting and funding.

- o Industry standards adoption and implementation of assessments.

- o Government regulatory requirements that may affect assessment scope.

Conduct Architecture Assessment: Methods & Strategies

1. Architecture expertise includes but is not limited to:

   o The architects' familiarity with the domain area can provide a more comprehensive assessment based on their experience.

   o Develop a clean and accurate assessment and identify the areas that need further clarification and validation to be addressed in the analysis phase.

   o Leverage technical and domain knowledge expertise from other sources to help provide multiple views and input into the assessment.

Conduct Architecture Assessment: Outputs

1. Architecture assessment document includes but is not limited to:

   o A formal document capturing the project assessment information and the initial scope, efforts and estimation of the size of the project and resource needs.

4.3 Architecture Analysis Processes

Architecture analysis is the second phase of the architecture management processes. It serves to determine the scope of the problems architects are trying to solve. Architects use architecture knowledge and techniques to assist them in the analysis. This helps fine tune the level of effort and estimation numbers that were established during the engagement phase. The analysis phase tends to be a fact finding and documentation journey. Architects collect extensive knowledge of the areas being investigated in order to select the best methods to tackle each problem and design issue, using architecture patterns and techniques. A considerable amount of time is spent during this phase to grasp all the different angles of looking at a problem with which they are confronted. Figure 4-7 illustrates a high level overview of the processes involved in the architecture analysis phase, including its associated inputs, methods & strategies, and outputs. The first process is 4.3.1 Conduct Requirements Analysis, the second process is 4.3.2 Conduct Risk & Impact Assessment, the third process is 4.3.3 Document Assumptions, and the fourth process is 4.3.4 Document Resources Requirements.

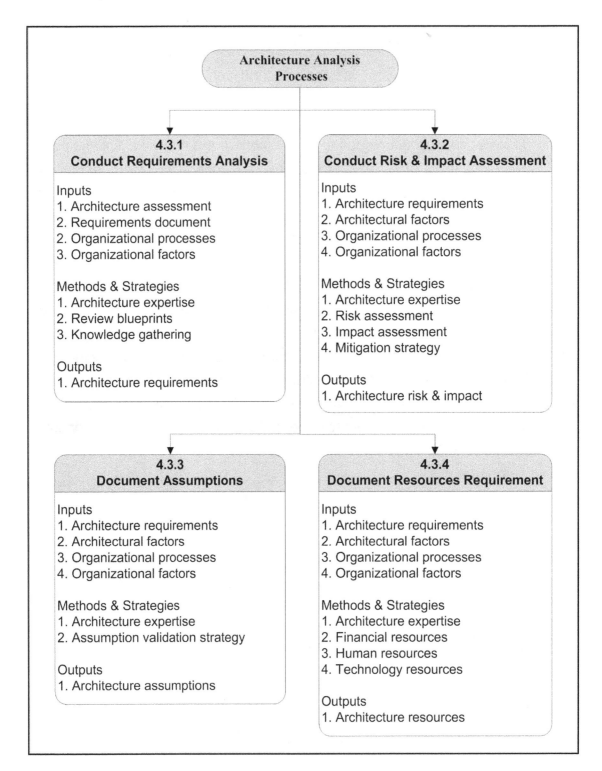

Figure 4-7. Architecture Analysis Processes Overview

Figure 4-8 illustrates the interaction diagram for the architecture analysis processes. The architecture assessment and organization specific processes contribute to the analysis processes by providing input such as architecture assessment documents, requirements, architectural factors, organizational processes and factors.

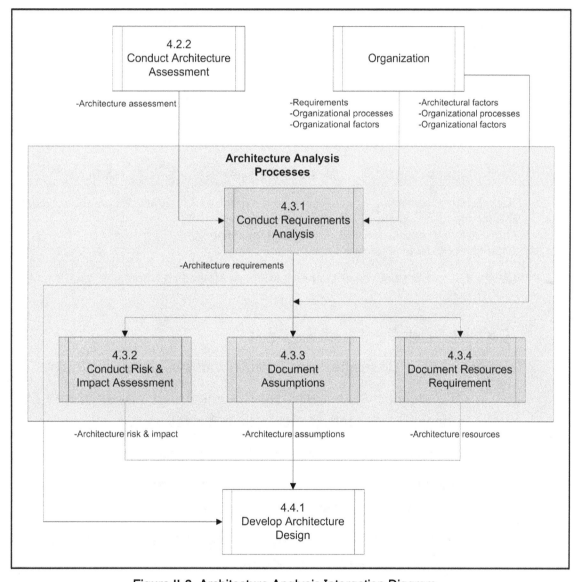

Figure 4-8. Architecture Analysis Interaction Diagram

4.3.1   Conduct Requirements Analysis

Conduct requirements analysis is a process to collect project information that has direct and indirect relationships to architecture decisions that will affect the design. This includes the type of interaction between the architecture and existing systems or components, integration requirements between upstream and downstream systems, and the required bill of materials and components that need to be built, purchased or assembled to construct the new system. The more information collected, the better the architects' understanding of what needs to be built and what impact it will have on the existing environment.

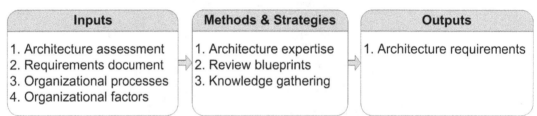

Figure 4-9. Conduct Requirements Analysis: Inputs, Methods & Strategies, and Outputs

Conduct Requirement Analysis: Inputs

1. Architecture assessment document includes but is not limited to:

   o The architecture assessment document that was produced from process 4.2.2 Conduct Architecture Assessment.

2. Requirements document includes but is not limited to:

   o Provides the architect with the means to map out how the architecture will satisfy such requirements.

   o Input to the architecture requirements to determine the scope and features that need to be analyzed.

3. Organizational processes include but are not limited to:

   o Company specific processes that contribute to the scope of the analysis.

   o Existing processes, documentation, and knowledge base to provide input and direction to analysis techniques.

4. Organizational factors include but are not limited to:

   o Organizational structure and culture that may affect accessibility to information.

   o Industry standards adoption and implementation for analysis methods.

   o Government regulatory requirements that affect the analysis scope.

Conduct Requirement Analysis: Methods & Strategies

1. Architecture expertise includes but is not limited to:

   o The architects' familiarity with the domain area will provide a more comprehensive analysis based on their experience.

   o Develop analysis documentation, alternatives and identify the areas that need further clarification and validation to be addressed in the design phase.

2. Review blueprints include but are not limited to:

   o Architecture blueprint should be a source for up-to-date and accurate information about how existing systems are architected and built.

   o Architects need to review existing blueprints to build a solid analysis and understanding of how the new requirements will impact existing designs.

o Blueprints will provide architects with guidance in what areas need to be analyzed to complete a comprehensive analysis that can lead to good design.

3. Knowledge gathering includes but is not limited to:

o Knowledge gathering provides architects with the information they need to complete a comprehensive analysis.

o Gathering, summarizing and synthesizing information that can be captured through existing documentation, verbal discussions, and analysis meeting notes.

Conduct Requirement Analysis: Outputs

1. Architecture requirements document includes but is not limited to:

o A formal document capturing the architecture requirements information to be used in the architecture design phase.

o The document represents the architects' understanding of the business requirements, translated into architecture terminology.

4.3.2   Conduct Risk & Impact Assessment

Conduct risk and impact assessment is the process of capturing and documenting the associated risks that have been identified as part of the analysis and the impact these risks have on existing systems and architecture. The risks and impacts collected are relevant to the architecture and need to be addressed, managed and mitigated by the architect. The risks and impacts can be rolled into the overall project management risks and impacts for reporting purposes.

Inputs	Methods & Strategies	Outputs
1. Architecture requirements 2. Architectural factors 3. Organizational processes 4. Organizational factors	1. Architecture expertise 2. Risk assessment 3. Impact assessment 4. Mitigation strategy	1. Architecture risk & impact

Figure 4-10. Conduct Risk & Impact Analysis: Inputs, Methods & Strategies, and Outputs

Conduct Risk & Impact Assessment: Inputs

1. Architecture requirements document includes but is not limited to:

   o The architecture requirements document that was produced from process 4.3.1 Conduct Requirements Analysis.

2. Architectural factors include but are not limited to:

   o Architectural best practices and techniques to manage and reduce risks and impacts.

   o Architectural templates that capture the risk and impact analysis.

   o Architecture risk and impact signing authority, depending on the risk and impact level.

   o Architecture communication processes for risks and impact reviews.

3. Organizational processes include but are not limited to:

   o Company specific processes that mandates how risks and impacts need to be reported and escalated.

   o Company specific processes that address who needs to sign off on the risks and their associated impact if they cannot be resolved or mitigated.

4. Organizational factors include but are not limited to:

- o Organizational structure and culture that may affect signing authority on risks and impacts.

- o Industry standards adoption and implementation to reduce risks and impact.

- o Government regulatory requirements that may require high risks and impacts to be reported.

Conduct Risk & Impact Assessment: Methods & Strategies

1. Architecture expertise includes but is not limited to:

- o The architects' familiarity with the domain area will provide a more comprehensive risk and impact assessment based on their experience.

- o The architects' prior experience will contribute to the speed of risk and impact identification. Similar projects that were implemented in the past may be a great source for reviewing what type of risks and impacts can be leveraged for the new implementation.

2. Risk assessment includes but is not limited to:

- o Architects can leverage their experience and use technical experts from domain area specialists to help them in assessing the risks identified and help categorize and rate the risks.

- o Architects can use risk assessment templates that can include architecture relevant information.

3. Impact assessment includes but is not limited to:

- o Architects can leverage their experiences and use technical experts from domain area specialists to help them in determining the impact to existing systems if the risks are not mitigated.

- o Architects can use impact assessment templates that can include architecture relevant information.

4. Mitigation strategy includes but is not limited to:

   o Architects can leverage their experience and use technical experts from domain area specialists to help them in creating mitigating and backup strategies for the risks and impacts identified.

   o Evaluate similar implementations that were completed in the past to come up with reusable mitigation strategies.

Conduct Risk & Impact Assessment: Outputs

1. Architecture risk and impact document includes but is not limited to:

   o A formal document capturing the architecture risks and impacts and how they will be mitigated to help improve project implementation success.

4.3.3   Document Assumptions

Document assumptions is a process for capturing and documenting the assumptions that have been identified as part of the analysis phase. The process also includes the development of plans to test and validate the assumptions. Assumption clarification is an important part of the nature of the architecture discipline and the personality of an architect. Architects try to identify and capture all the unknowns to close the gap for any grey areas that may exist between the known and unknown. Architects work hard to make the design very clear and document the assumptions that need to be validated and tested for further clarification.

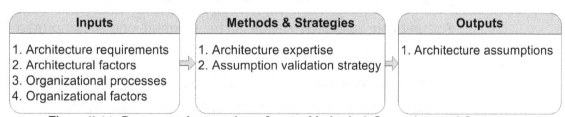

Inputs	Methods & Strategies	Outputs
1. Architecture requirements 2. Architectural factors 3. Organizational processes 4. Organizational factors	1. Architecture expertise 2. Assumption validation strategy	1. Architecture assumptions

Figure 4-11. Document Assumptions: Inputs, Methods & Strategies, and Outputs

Document Assumptions: Inputs

1. Architecture requirements document includes but is not limited to:

   o The architecture requirements document that was produced from process 4.3.1 Conduct Requirements Analysis.

2. Architectural factors include but are not limited to:

   o Architectural best practices and techniques to document, manage and validate assumptions.

3. Organizational processes include but are not limited to:

   o Company specific processes that mandate how assumptions need to be reported, resolved or escalated.

4. Organizational factors include but are not limited to:

   o Organizational structure and culture that may affect assumptions.

   o Industry standards that may provide tools to validate assumptions.

Document Assumptions: Methods & Strategies

1. Architecture expertise includes but is not limited to:

   o Due to familiarity with the area, the architects will understand how assumptions can be validated based on experience and knowledge.

   o Develop clear assumptions and identify the ways in which they can be tested and validated during the design phase.

2. Assumption validation strategy includes but is not limited to:

   o Assumption validation needs to be planned and incorporated in the overall project plan.

   o Some assumptions can be validated early in the design and others have to be delayed to the time of implementation.

   o The associated risks and impact of the untested assumptions need to be addressed and managed.

<u>Document Assumptions: Outputs</u>

1. Architecture assumptions document includes but is not limited to:

   o A formal document capturing the architecture assumptions and their testing validation strategies to help improve the project's implementation success and reduce the unknowns that may be associated with higher risk and impact.

4.3.4 Document Resources Requirement

Document resources requirement is a process for capturing and documenting resource needs. This includes financial needs, human needs, and technology required to establish the architecture design and implement the architecture. Document resources also includes the components and bill of material that are required to complete the project. This document can be extremely valuable to the project and Project Managers in that it validates the financial and human commitment of the business to bring this project to a good start and clean finish.

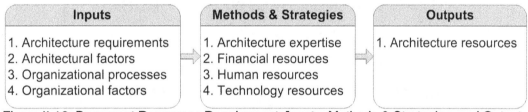

Inputs	Methods & Strategies	Outputs
1. Architecture requirements 2. Architectural factors 3. Organizational processes 4. Organizational factors	1. Architecture expertise 2. Financial resources 3. Human resources 4. Technology resources	1. Architecture resources

Figure 4-12. Document Resources Requirement: Inputs, Methods & Strategies, and Outputs

<u>Document Resources Requirement: Inputs</u>

1. Architecture requirements document includes but is not limited to:

   o The architecture requirements document that was produced from process 4.3.1 Conduct Requirements Analysis.

2. Architectural factors include but are not limited to:

- o Architectural best practices and techniques to include pre-defined resources needs.

- o Existing architecture documentation may help identify resource needs from similar projects previously completed.

3. Organizational processes include but are not limited to:

- o Company specific processes that mandates how resources are used and deployed.

4. Organizational factors include but are not limited to:

- o Organizational structure and culture that may affect how resources are managed.

- o Industry standards that may affect how technology resources are used.

- o Government influence on financial resources such as grants and funding that has to be spent by a specific time.

Document resources requirement: Methods & Strategies

1. Architecture expertise includes but is not limited to:

- o The architects' experience from previous projects can determine the required resources needed.

2. Financial resources include but are not limited to:

- o The required financial commitment to invest in technology, hardware, software, and services.

3. Human resources include but are not limited to:

- o The human technical expertise required to successfully deliver the project.

- o Architects work with the project manager to plan how to use the technical IT resources required for the project.

- o Leverage internal and external human knowledge and expertise.

4. Technology resources include but are not limited to:

- o The architecture component building block and bill of material for all technological requirements such as hardware, software, network, systems, and services.

- o The architects' understanding of how the technology components fit together will assist the Project Manager in determining the technology needs and dependencies.

Document resources requirement: Outputs

1. Architecture resources document includes but is not limited to:

- o A formal document capturing the architecture resources required to fund, develop and implement the desired architecture design of the project.

4.4 Architecture Design Processes

Architecture design is the third phase of the architecture management processes. It serves to determine the design options and architecture patterns that will be employed. The analysis conducted in the second phase will be used as input in the design process. In this phase, architects utilize their experience and recall how similar problems were solved in the past. They determine how design and architecture will meet the business requirements in the most efficient and effective way. A considerable amount of time is spent during this phase to grasp all the different design options and alternatives. It is much easier to detect design errors at this level—before a single line of code is written or any system configuration is done. If the design is prepared exceptionally well, the implementation phase will go smoothly and the support efforts and maintenance costs for the system will be reduced. Figure 4-13 illustrates a high level overview of the processes involved in the architecture design phase, including its associated inputs, methods & strategies, and outputs. The first process is 4.4.1 Develop Architecture Design, the second process is 4.4.2 Evaluate Design Alternatives, and the third process is 4.4.3 Approve Architecture Design.

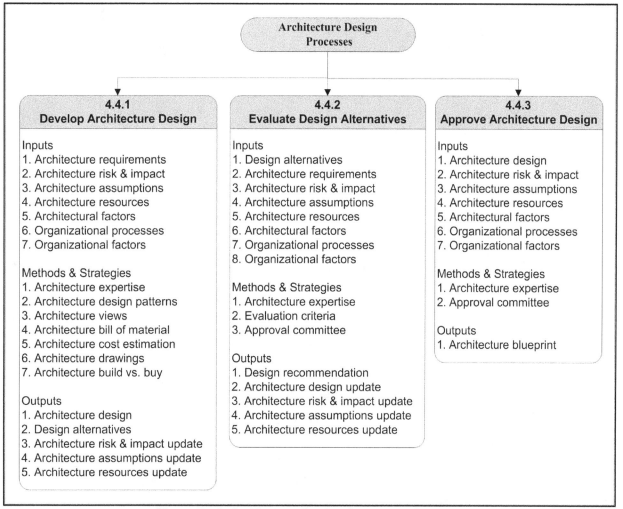

Figure 4-13. Architecture Design Processes Overview

Figure 4-14 illustrates the interaction diagram for the architecture design processes. The architecture requirements, risk & impact, assumptions, resources, and organization specific processes contribute to the input of the design process.

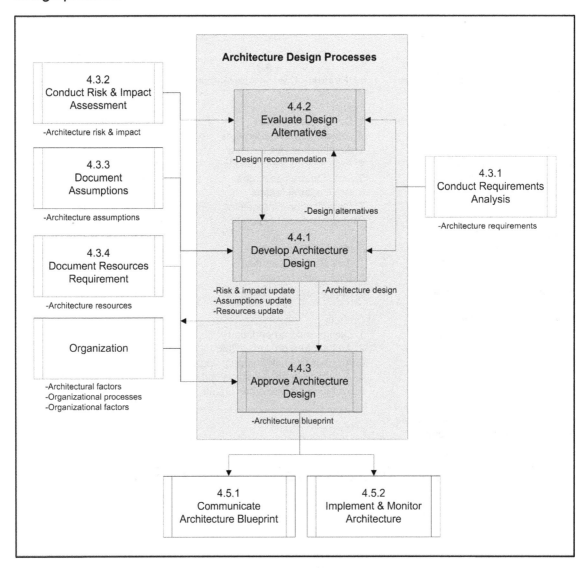

Figure 4-14. Architecture Design Interaction Diagram

4.4.1 Develop Architecture Design

Develop architecture design is a process of translating the business requirements, architecture requirements and analysis into design components. The design will define how the layout of the system will be architected. Previous experience, design patterns, and industry standards may influence how a system is designed. There may exist more than one design option to solve the business problem and meet the business requirements. Multiple factors may influence how the architect uses the systematic approach to determine which design alternatives to go with.

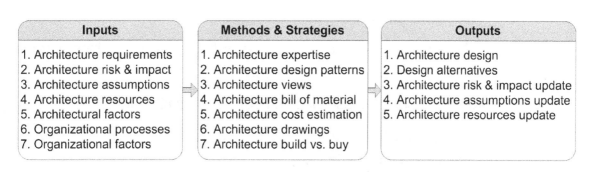

Inputs	Methods & Strategies	Outputs
1. Architecture requirements	1. Architecture expertise	1. Architecture design
2. Architecture risk & impact	2. Architecture design patterns	2. Design alternatives
3. Architecture assumptions	3. Architecture views	3. Architecture risk & impact update
4. Architecture resources	4. Architecture bill of material	4. Architecture assumptions update
5. Architectural factors	5. Architecture cost estimation	5. Architecture resources update
6. Organizational processes	6. Architecture drawings	
7. Organizational factors	7. Architecture build vs. buy	

Figure 4-15. Develop Architecture Design: Inputs, Methods & Strategies, and Outputs

Develop Architecture Design: Inputs

1. Architecture requirements document includes but is not limited to:

   o The architecture requirements document that was produced from process 4.3.1 Conduct Requirements Analysis.

2. Architecture risk and impact document includes but is not limited to:

   o The architecture risk & impact document that was produced from process 4.3.2 Conduct Risk & Impact Assessment.

3. Architecture assumptions document includes but not is limited to:

   o The architecture assumptions document that was produced from process 4.3.3 Document Assumptions.

4. Architecture resources document includes but is not limited to:

   o The architecture resources document that was produced from process 4.3.4 Document Resources Requirement.

5. Architecture factors include but are not limited to:

   o Architectural best practices and techniques that may influence design options.

   o Architectural standards, frameworks, processes that may affect design alternatives.

   o Architecture governance processes that need to be incorporated into the design approval processes.

6. Organizational processes include but are not limited to:

   o Company specific processes that may affect resources and may impact the architected design.

7. Organizational factors include but are not limited to:

   o Organizational structure and culture that may affect how resources are allocated and may affect architecture design alternatives.

   o Industry standards that may affect how design patterns are used.

   o Government influence on financial resources such as grants and funding that must be spent by a specific time and may influence design alternatives.

Develop Architecture Design: Methods & Strategies

1. Architecture expertise includes but not is limited to:

- o The architects' experience from pervious projects can be leveraged to come up with multiple design options.

- o The architects' expertise in the domain areas. The associated design patterns may influence the architecture design.

2. Architecture design patterns include but are not limited to:

- o Architecture design patterns are proven, tested and commonly used by organizations. Such design patterns may include publish/subscribe, message exchange patterns, change data capture, and data discovery.

3. Architecture views include but are not limited to:

- o The different architecture views give the architect the ability to slice the architecture design into multiple angles. This will strengthen the structural integrity of the design by causing the examination of each view for design consideration.

- o Philippe Kruchten 4+1 architecture views is a famous model that illustrates the need for a logical view, development view, process view, physical view and scenarios.

4. Architecture bill of material includes but is not limited to:

- o Required hardware, network, servers, and computer components.

- o Required services that need to be coordinated with other teams.

- o Required software packages and their associated licensing needs.

- o Required physical space, datacenter floor space, heating & cooling needs.

- o Required physical building security needs.

- o Required application, system, or data needs.

5. Architecture cost estimation includes but is not limited to:

   o A detailed estimate of the bill of material includes both hard cost and soft cost. Hard cost includes the purchasing of hardware and software. Soft cost includes people's time on projects.

   o Cost may play a role in influencing architecture decisions. Therefore, good estimation is key in making sure that architecture decision alternatives are compared fairly.

6. Architecture drawings include but are not limited to:

   o Architecture drawings provide an abstract view of the system design. They are made in order to communicate the system components and their interaction in a simple and easy to understand, visual form. "A picture is worth a thousand words."

7. Architecture build vs. buy includes but is not limited to:

   o Architects always need to evaluate the build vs. buy approach.

   o If there are components that can be purchased and can be integrated into existing architecture design, it would make sense to buy and not reinvent the wheel. However, in some cases, it may make more sense to build the system from scratch.

   o Support cost, time to market, development efforts, and the overall total cost of ownership play a role in the buy or build decision.

Develop Architecture Design: Outputs

1. Architecture design document includes but is not limited to:

   o A formal document capturing the architecture design required to implement the desired architecture for the project.

2. Design alternative document includes but is not limited to:

   o A formal document capturing the architecture design alternatives that need to be evaluated. These must be based on specific criteria in order to come up with the best design that meets the requirements.

3. Architecture risk & impact update includes but is not limited to:

   o Update to the risk & impact document based on the architecture design.

4. Architecture assumptions update includes but is not limited to:

   o Update to the assumptions document based on the architecture design.

5. Architecture resources update includes but is not limited to:

   o Update to the resources document based on the architecture design.

4.4.2   Evaluate Design Alternatives

Evaluate design alternatives is a process that allows architects to document multiple design options and their advantages and disadvantages. This process provides a neutral analysis and measures the design options based on the criteria provided to create an unbiased decision. This process builds confidence in the design process and makes sure that multiple views and angles have been addressed in the best interest of the organization. A design recommendation is produced from this process and an approval committee is involved in reviewing the design alternatives. Architects have to keep in mind that architecture design decisions for alternatives are time and information dependent. This means that based on the available information at the time of analysis the recommended alternatives are selected.

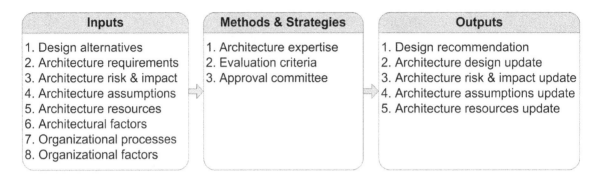

Figure 4-16. Evaluate Design Alternatives: Inputs, Methods & Strategies, and Outputs

Evaluate Design Alternatives: Inputs

1. Design alternatives document includes but is not limited to:

   o The architecture design alternatives document that was produced from process 4.4.1 Develop Architecture Design.

2. Architectural requirements include but are not limited to:

   o The architecture requirements document that was produced from process 4.3.1 Conduct Requirements Analysis.

3. Architectural risk & impact includes but is not limited to:

   o The architecture risk & impact document that was produced from process 4.3.2 Conduct Risk & Impact Assessment.

4. Architectural assumptions include but are not limited to:

   o The architecture assumptions document that was produced from process 4.3.3 Document Assumptions.

5. Architectural resources include but are not limited to:

   o The architecture resources document that was produced from process 4.3.4 Document Resources Requirement.

6. Architectural factors include but are not limited to:

   o Architectural best practices and techniques that may influence design options.

- o Architectural standards, frameworks, processes that may affect design alternatives.
- o Architecture governance processes that need to be incorporated into the design approval processes.

7. Organizational processes include but are not limited to:

- o Company specific processes that may affect resources and may impact the architected design.

8. Organizational factors include but are not limited to:

- o Organizational structure and culture that may affect how resources are allocated and may affect architecture design alternatives.
- o Industry standards that may affect how design patterns are used.
- o Government influence on financial resources, such as grants and funding that has to be spent by a specific time, and may affect design alternatives.

Evaluate Design Alternatives: Methods & Strategies

1. Architecture expertise includes but is not limited to:

- o The architects' experience from previous projects can be leveraged and architects can recommend between the multiple design options.
- o The architects' expertise in the domain areas and their associated design patterns may influence the architecture design alternative recommendation.

2. Evaluation criteria includes but is not limited to:

- o A set of criteria that will have a weighted scale to determine how each design option is measured.

- o Sample evaluation criteria may include cost, flexibility, time to deliver, development efforts required, strategic direction, and technology direction.

3. Architecture approval committee includes but is not limited to:

- o A group of individuals that will review the design alternatives and the architects' analysis based on the weighted criteria. The approval committee may approve or reject the architects' recommendation.

- o Approval committee members are typically made of other architects and the Enterprise/Chief architect. Depending on the size and scope of the project, more members may be added or removed based on the organization's architecture approval and governance structure.

Evaluate Design Alternatives: Outputs

1. Design recommendation includes but is not limited to:

- o A formal document capturing the architecture design alternatives, recommendation, and rationale based on the evaluation criteria.

2. Architecture design document updates include but are not limited to:

- o Update to the architecture design document based on the architecture design alternative choice.

3. Architecture risk and impact document updates include but are not limited to:

- o Update to the risk & impact document based on the architecture design alternative choice.

4. Architecture assumptions document updates include but are not limited to:

- o Update to the assumptions document based on the architecture design alternative choice.

5. Architecture resources document updates includes but is not limited to:

   o Update to the resources document based on the architecture design alternative choice.

4.4.3 Approve Architecture Design

Approve architecture design is a formal process for architects to bring forward their architecture design to the architecture committee for analysis, review, critique, approval or rejection. This process builds a stronger architectural discipline by making architects aware of the corporate policies, processes, standards, framework and governance requirements. This process also acts as knowledge sharing of new design patterns and techniques to be reviewed by the approval committee. This can also be a formal mentoring and evaluation opportunity for architects by more senior and influential architects in the organization.

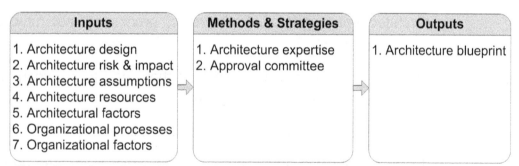

Inputs	Methods & Strategies	Outputs
1. Architecture design 2. Architecture risk & impact 3. Architecture assumptions 4. Architecture resources 5. Architectural factors 6. Organizational processes 7. Organizational factors	1. Architecture expertise 2. Approval committee	1. Architecture blueprint

Figure 4-17. Approve Architecture Design: Inputs, Methods & Strategies, and Outputs

Approve Architecture Design: Inputs

1. Architecture design document includes but is not limited to:

   o The architecture design document that was produced from process 4.4.1 Develop Architecture Design.

2. Architectural risk & impact includes but is not limited to:

   o The architecture risk & impact document that was produced from process 4.3.2 Conduct Risk & Impact Assessment.

3. Architectural assumptions include but are not limited to:

   o The architecture assumptions document that was produced from process 4.3.3 Document Assumptions.

4. Architectural resources include but are not limited to:

   o The architecture resources document that was produced from process 4.3.4 Document Resources Requirement.

5. Architectural factors include but are not limited to:

   o Architectural best practices and techniques that may influence the design approval decision.

   o Architectural standards, frameworks, processes that may affect design approval.

   o Architecture governance processes that need to be incorporated into the design approval processes.

6. Organizational processes include but are not limited to:

   o Company specific processes that may affect resources and may impact the architected design.

7. Organizational factors include but are not limited to:

   o Organizational structure and culture that may affect how resources are allocated and may affect architecture design approval.

- o Industry standards that may affect how the proposed architecture design is compliant with industry standards.

- o Government regulatory requirements may affect the approval process.

Approve Architecture Design: Methods & Strategies

1. Architecture expertise includes but is not limited to:

   - o The architects' experience from pervious projects and interaction with the architecture governance board will expedite the approval process if they are very familiar with what is required from the approval board.

   - o The architects' expertise in the domain areas and their associated design patterns will build strong confidence in the credibility of the design.

2. Architecture approval committee includes but is not limited to:

   - o A group of individuals that will review the architecture design and supporting documents.

   - o Approval committee members are typically made up of other architects and the Enterprise/Chief architect. Depending on the size and scope of the project, more members may be added or removed based on the organization's architecture approval and governance structure.

Approve architecture design: Outputs

1. Architecture blueprint document includes but is not limited to:

   - o A formal approved document capturing the architecture design/blueprint required to implement the desired architecture for the project.

4.5 Architecture Implementation Processes

Architecture implementation is the fourth phase of the architecture management processes. Architects will take the architecture blueprint and work with different teams such as developers, testers, infrastructure personnel, system administrators, and DBAs and guide them through the implementation of the design. IT architects play a key role in mentoring and monitoring the development efforts in conjunction with the project manager. Architects will guide the technical components and will ensure that the project progression is on track. Any design issues or problems that might surface during the implementing phase should be brought up to the architects' attention to deal with and solve. Figure 4-18 illustrates a high level overview of the processes involved in the architecture implementation phase including its associated inputs, methods & strategies, and outputs. The first process is 4.5.1 Communicate Architecture Blueprint, the second process is 4.5.2 Implement & Monitor Architecture.

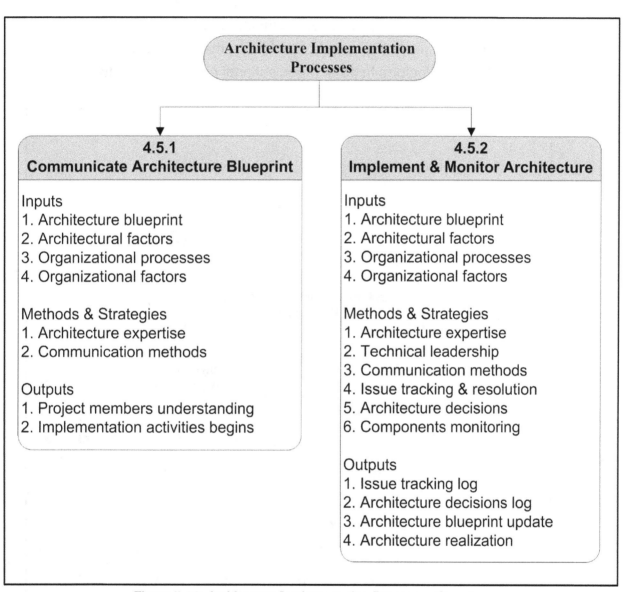

Figure 4-18. Architecture Implementation Processes Overview

Figure 4-19 illustrates the interaction diagram for the architecture implementation processes. The approved architecture design and organization specific processes contribute to the implementation processes by providing inputs such as the architecture blueprint document, architectural factors, organisational processes and factors.

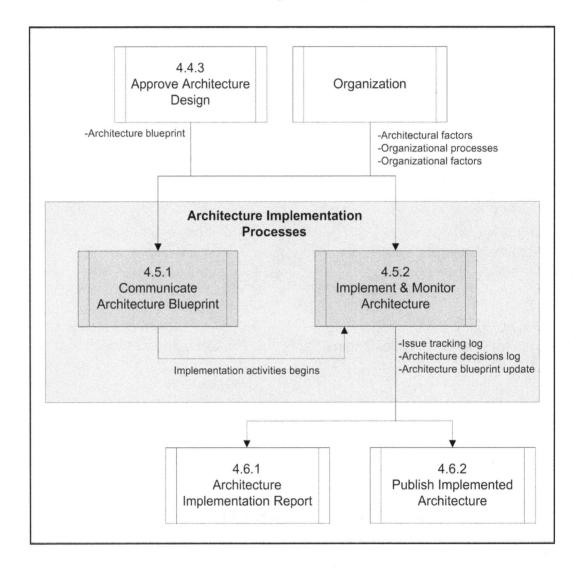

Figure 4-19. Architecture Implementation Interaction Diagram

4.5.1   Communicate Architecture Blueprint

Communicate architecture blueprint is a process of sharing the approved architecture blueprint with project team members such as developers, technical leads and others in order for them to start working on the detailed design, and begin the development and implementation activities. The communication plan may include a project team meeting where the architect walks through the approved design with all participants to make sure they are aware of the different components that need to be built. This process from an architect's perspective marks the beginning of the implementation efforts required to make this architecture design a reality.

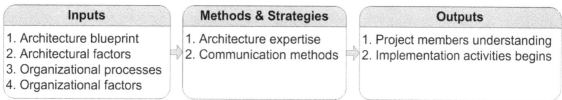

Inputs	Methods & Strategies	Outputs
1. Architecture blueprint 2. Architectural factors 3. Organizational processes 4. Organizational factors	1. Architecture expertise 2. Communication methods	1. Project members understanding 2. Implementation activities begins

Figure 4-20. Communicate Architecture Blueprint: Inputs, Methods & Strategies, and Outputs

Communicate Architecture Blueprint: Inputs

1. Architecture blueprint document includes but is not limited to:

    o   The approved architecture blueprint document that was produced from process 4.4.3 Approve Architecture Design.

2. Architecture factors include but are not limited to:

    o   Architecture best practices and techniques to that may influence the communication methods.

3. Organizational processes include but are not limited to:

    o   Company specific communication processes that may affect how the architecture blueprint will be communicated.

4. Organizational factors include but are not limited to:

   o Organizational structure and culture that may affect how communication processes are delivered.

Communicate Architecture Blueprint: Methods & Strategies

1. Architecture expertise includes but is not limited to:

   o The architects' expertise and knowledge in the domain area and their relationship with different teams within the organization may influence how the architecture design will be delivered. Some architects may prefer a one-on-one with technical leads and developers to walk them through the design. Others may prefer a general team meeting to present the design.

2. Communication methods include but are not limited to:

   o E-mail communication to present the approved design to the project team.

   o A team meeting with project members to walk through the architecture design.

   o One-on-one meetings with technical leads and developers who will take the architecture design to the next level to produce detail designs.

   o Publishing the blueprints to a corporate intranet webpage specific to the project for knowledge sharing.

Communicate Architecture Blueprint: Outputs

1. Project members understanding includes but is not limited to:

   o A general understanding by the project team members of the architecture design and how the individual components contribute to the overall project.

2. Implementation activities begins includes but is not limited to:

o A signal that marks the beginning of the development and implementation activities that will make the architecture design a reality.

4.5.2 Implement & Monitor Architecture

Implement & monitor architecture is a process that supports the development and implementation phase of the architecture. The architect takes a technical leadership role to lead the development and technical components. The architect is responsible for resolving technical issues that are related to the architecture. Architects use this phase to test and validate the architecture blueprint based on information and feedback coming from the development and technical teams. A good architecture design should be straightforward during the implementation phase. However, sometimes with less experienced architects, design flaws will show in this phase. Signs of design weakness result in a series of problems. Logging the issues and architecture decisions made during implementation are critical for future process and design improvements. The after-implemented review and report will assess the approved design against the implemented design and determine the gap variance between both.

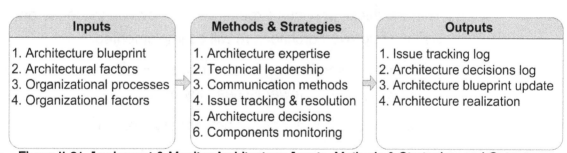

Inputs	Methods & Strategies	Outputs
1. Architecture blueprint	1. Architecture expertise	1. Issue tracking log
2. Architectural factors	2. Technical leadership	2. Architecture decisions log
3. Organizational processes	3. Communication methods	3. Architecture blueprint update
4. Organizational factors	4. Issue tracking & resolution	4. Architecture realization
	5. Architecture decisions	
	6. Components monitoring	

Figure 4-21. Implement & Monitor Architecture: Inputs, Methods & Strategies, and Outputs

Implement & Monitor Architecture: Inputs

1. Architecture blueprint document includes but is not limited to:

   o The approved architecture blueprint document that was produced from process 4.4.3 Approve Architecture Design.

2. Architecture factors include but are not limited to:

   o Architectural best practices and techniques that may influence how the approved architecture gets implemented.

   o Architectural standards, frameworks, and processes that may affect architecture implementation.

3. Organizational processes include but are not limited to:

   o Company specific processes that may affect resources and may impact the architecture implementation.

4. Organizational factors include but are not limited to:

   o Organizational structure and culture that may affect how resources are allocated and may affect architecture implementation.

Implement & Monitor Architecture: Methods & Strategies

1. Architecture expertise includes but is not limited to:

   o The architects' previous experience will have an influence on how well the approved architecture will be implemented.

   o The more experience the architect gains, the easier the implementation and fewer issues may arise.

2. Technical leadership includes but not is limited to:

   o The architect provides technical leadership and guidance through the entire project implementation phase.

   o The architect should be the go-to person for any issues and design questions that come up during the implementation.

- o The architect needs to be alert and monitor each phase and sub-phase of the implementation to resolve issues very quickly.

3. Communication methods include but are not limited to:

- o The implementation and monitoring phase tends to be overwhelmingly packed with development activities and moving parts which create tension and stress. Effective and efficient communication is key in making sure that things do not fall through the cracks and get dropped.

- o Email communication, phone conversations, face to face meetings and group meetings are very common.

4. Issue tracking & resolution includes but is not limited to:

- o Architecture design issues need to be tracked and documented and need to include the resolutions to the issues.

5. Architecture decisions include but are not limited to:

- o Architecture decisions made during the implementation and monitoring phase need to be captured and logged. Some situations may require approval, depending on the level of risk and impact to the project.

6. Components monitoring includes but is not limited to:

- o Architects need to monitor the architecture as a whole as well as each component of the architecture as it is being built, integrated and assembled.

- o This allows architects to check for any constraints and design incompatibilities that may have been missed during the design phase.

- o Team members may have worked on a single or multiple components, but the accountability remains with the architect to figure out how to integrate the components.

- o Architects are knowledgeable about how design components fit and work together.

Implement & Monitor Architecture: Outputs

1. Issue tracking log includes but is not limited to:

   - o A formal document that captures the architecture issues and resolution during the implementation and monitoring phase to be used for the post project architecture review and report.

2. Architecture decisions log includes but is not limited to:

   - o A formal document that captures the architecture decisions and approval during the implementation and monitoring phase to be used for the post project architecture review and report.

3. Architecture blueprint update includes but is not limited to:

   - o Updates to the architecture blueprint if the design had to be altered due to architecture issues or decisions during implementation.

4. Architecture realization includes but is not limited to:

   - o Marks the end of the implementation and monitoring phase and the beginning of the realization of the implemented architecture.

   - o A working system that resembles the architecture.

4.6 Architecture Realization Processes

Architecture realization is the fifth and last phase of the architecture management processes. Architects finalize any documentation for the system and educate support teams about the implemented design. Architects submit all documentation to the architecture repository and provide a final report to the AMO. The architecture documentation and blueprints of the system needs to be a living document and any changes to the system after the project is completed will need to be updated. Project status and report feedback need to be communicated to the bigger architecture practice initiatives, such as enterprise architecture programs. Figure 4-22 illustrates a high level overview of the processes involved in the architecture realization phase including its associated inputs, methods & strategies, and outputs. The first process is 4.6.1 Architecture Implementation Report, the second process is 4.6.2 Publish Implemented Architecture.

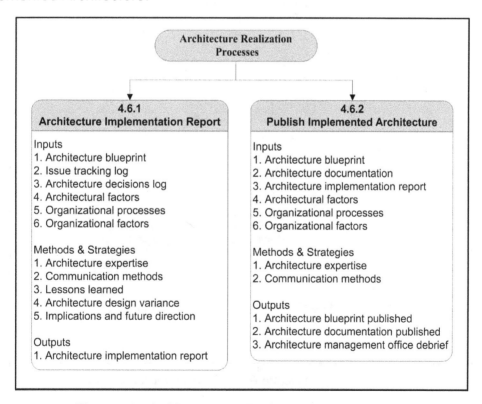

Figure 4-22. Architecture Realization Processes Overview

Figure 4-23 illustrates the interaction diagram for the architecture realization processes. The implement & monitor architecture and organization specific processes contribute to the realization processes by providing inputs such as architecture blueprint document, issues tracking log, architecture decisions log, architectural factors, organizational processes and factors.

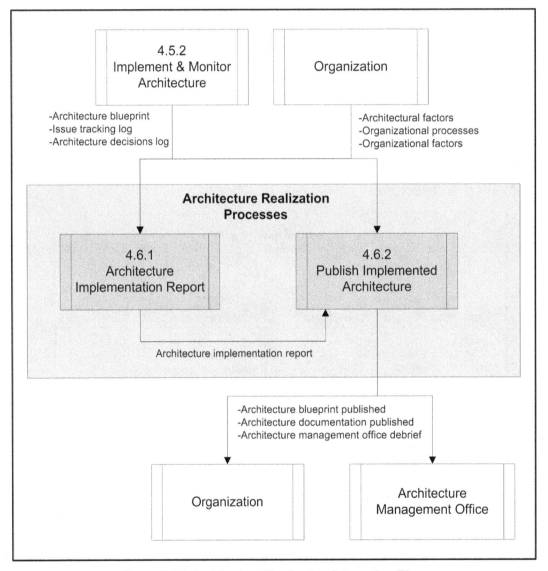

Figure 4-23. Architecture Realization Interaction Diagram

4.6.1   Architecture Implementation Report

Architecture implementation report is the process of summarizing the architecture implementation results, including any design issues or decisions that were faced during the implementation and monitoring phase. This is a necessary step in building the architect's career and knowledge and the AMO maturity and development. Analyzing the lessons learned, issues faced, and challenges that were overcome is critical for the success and growth of the architecture practice. The AMO management will prepare the report and distribute the acquired knowledge to the rest of the AMO members. The report is valuable in measuring the architects' competency and will determine if there areas of improvement necessary for the architect and future architecture projects.

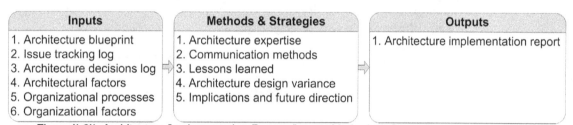

Figure 4-24. Architecture Implementation Report: Inputs, Methods & Strategies, and Outputs

Architecture Implementation Report: Inputs

1. Architecture blueprint document includes but is not limited to:

    o   The approved architecture blueprint document that was produced from process 4.4.3 Approve Architecture Design.

2. Issue tracking log includes but is not limited to:

    o   The issue tracking log that was produced from process 4.5.2 Implement & Monitor Architecture.

3. Architecture decisions log includes but is not limited to:

- o The architecture decisions log that was produced from process 4.5.2 Implement & Monitor Architecture.

4. Architecture factors include but are not limited to:

- o Architectural best practices and techniques that may influence how the report needs to be structured and shared.

- o Architectural standards, frameworks, and processes that may affect architecture reporting requirements.

5. Organizational processes include but are not limited to:

- o Company specific processes that may affect resources and may impact the architecture report development and distribution.

6. Organizational factors include but are not limited to:

- o Organizational structure and culture that may affect how the architecture report is accepted.

Architecture Implementation Report: Methods & Strategies

1. Architecture expertise document includes but is not limited to:

- o The architects' previous experience will have an influence on how the report will be viewed and shared.

- o The more experience the architect gains, the easier the implementation. The architect will face fewer issues and the quality of the report will be better.

2. Communication methods include but are not limited to:

- o The implementation report needs to be reviewed by the AMO and other architects for lessons learned and for rating the architecture implementation.

- o Email communication and/or a formal review process can be conducted by the AMO to review the project report.

- o Architects may choose to do a presentation to the AMO team to review the project report.

3. Lessons learned document includes but is not limited to:

   - o Lessons learned is a great tool for capturing and sharing what went correctly or badly in the project. Architects can learn from each other what was done successfully, as well as avoid making similar mistakes.

4. Architecture design variance includes but is not limited to:

   - o Architecture design variance is a measurement of how far the actual implementation strayed from the originally approved architecture design.

   - o Experienced architects will likely have a small variance, which means that the designed architecture was fully implemented without any changes, issues or updates. However, less experienced architects may have a large variance between what was designed and what was implemented.

   - o AMO needs to measure the variances and rate the architects' experience and use the results as input for the architects' performance and career development needs.

5. Implications and future direction include but are not limited to:

   - o Architects need to highlight the implications and future direction of new design patterns or technologies used in the implementation that others can learn from.

   - o Architects need to document the areas that have design components that were not implemented due to factors outside the control of the architect. The reasons, implications and how each particular issue needs to be solved in the future are very important for the growth of the architecture practice.

o Knowledge builds on previous knowledge and architects will take the organization one step forward by highlighting how the implemented project contributes to knowledge.

<u>Architecture Implementation Report: Outputs</u>

1. Architecture implementation report includes but is not limited to:

o A formal architecture implementation report document capturing the architecture lessons learned, issues log, decisions log, and other important factors that will contribute to the growth of the architect and the AMO from the experience gained in the implementation.

4.6.2   Publish Implemented Architecture

Publish implemented architecture is a process of formally publishing the architecture blueprint and associated documents for the organization. This helps in building a repository of architecture artifacts and becomes a source of knowledge for systems documentation. Any future modification to the system can benefit from the published architecture documents as evidence of what the system does and how it was constructed.

Figure 4-25. Publish Implemented Architecture: Inputs, Methods & Strategies, and Outputs

<u>Publish Implemented Architecture: Inputs</u>

1. Architecture blueprint document includes but is not limited to:

- The approved architecture blueprint document that was produced from process 4.4.3 Approve Architecture Design.

2. Architecture documentation includes but not is limited to:

- All other architecture documentation such as requirements, risk & impact, assumptions and resources.

3. Architecture implementation report includes but is not limited to:

- The architecture implementation report document that was produced from process 4.6.1 Architecture Implementation Report.

4. Architectural factors include but are not limited to:

- Architectural best practices and techniques that may influence how the report needs to be structured and shared.

- Architectural standards, frameworks, and processes that may affect architecture publishing requirements.

5. Organizational processes include but are not limited to:

- Company specific processes that may affect architecture publishing requirements.

6. Organizational factors include but are not limited to:

- Organizational structure and culture that may affect architecture publishing methods.

Publish Implemented Architecture: Methods & Strategies

1. Architecture expertise includes but is not limited to:

- The architects' previous experience will have an influence on how the publications will be viewed and shared.

- The more experience the architect gains, the easier the implementation and fewer issues that they may face, and the better the report and publishing quality.

2. Communication methods includes but is not limited to:

- o The architecture documentation needs to be reviewed by the AMO for completeness.

- o Email communication and publishing the documents to a shared drive or portal intranet where it is easily accessible to others for knowledge sharing.

Publish Implemented Architecture: Outputs

1. Architecture blueprint published includes but is not limited to:

   - o The architecture blueprint documents published to an organization specific destination that can be accessible to others for knowledge sharing.

2. Architecture documentation published includes but is not limited to:

   - o All architecture documents published to an organization specific destination that can be accessible to others for knowledge sharing.

3. Architecture management office debrief includes but is not limited to:

   - o A formal debrief by the architect to the AMO, highlighting the project report and documents.

CHAPTER 5

PROJECT MANAGEMENT INTEGRATION

IT architects and project managers play a key role in delivering successful IT projects. The success of projects can be influenced by how well projects are being managed from a project management methodology perspective. Their success can also be influenced by how IT architecture processes and methodologies are being used. Integrating processes between two major disciplines, IT architecture and project management, is critical to the coordination and implementation of IT projects.

This chapter will establish the knowledge required to integrate IT architecture management and project management processes and how process integration benefits organizations. This section is broken down as follows:

5.1 Project Management Integration Overview
5.2 Process Integration Mapping

5.1 Project Management Integration Overview

Information technology has changed the way business is being conducted in today's world. The complexity and advancement in business processes that are required to support organizational needs, have put tremendous pressure on leveraging new technology capabilities. Organizations are investing significant amounts of time, effort and funds in designing and building complex IT systems to support their strategic business direction. In order to reduce risks and increase project success rates, organizations are investing in and establishing formal disciplines such as IT architecture, project management, quality assurance, and others. These initiatives can support the organizations' IT implementations and operational needs. The next few pages will focus on developing an overview of project management and IT architecture, defining terms and concepts associated with the two disciplines, and summarizing the benefits of integrating the processes.

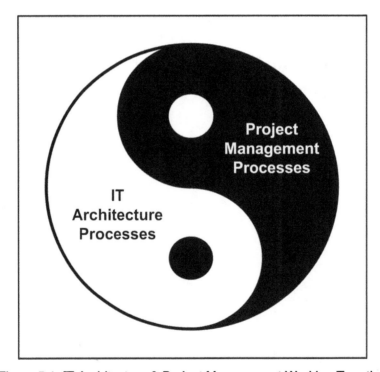

Figure 5-1. IT Architecture & Project Management Working Together

5.1.1   Project Management Discipline

<u>Project Management Institute:</u>

Project Management Institute (PMI) is a global leader and professional association for the project management profession. PMI offers a wide range of services dedicated to project management advancement. PMI services include but are not limited to development of standards, research, education, publication and certification.   For more information, refer to the *PMBOK® Guide,* 4th edition, and the Project Management Institute (www.pmi.org).

<u>Project Management:</u>

Project management focuses on satisfying project requirements through the use and implementation of knowledge, skills, tools and techniques for project activities.

<u>Project Manager:</u>

A person assigned by the organization to implement project management processes and methodologies to satisfy project objectives.

<u>*PMBOK® Guide*:</u>

Project Management Body Of Knowledge (*PMBOK® Guide)* is a recognized standard that includes processes, methods and generally accepted practices for the project management profession.

5.1.2   IT Architecture Discipline

<u>Architecture Management Institute:</u>

Architecture Management Institute (AMI) is an organization focused on the education, research, publication, training and certification for IT architecture management. AMI's primary focus is to increase the awareness and importance of IT architecture so it becomes and continues to be an integral part of IT project delivery methodologies.   Refer to Chapter 1, Section 1.1 for more details.

<u>IT Architecture:</u>

IT architecture in its generic form is defined as the art and science of designing and building information technology systems and other technology components such as hardware, software, application, network, infrastructure, security, data and information. Refer to Chapter 1, Section 1.5 for more details.

<u>IT Architecture Management:</u>

IT architecture management establishes knowledge, tools, processes, and techniques to define how IT architecture gets implemented. Refer to Chapter 2, 3 and 4 for more details on the IT architect role, the AMO and architecture management processes, respectively.

<u>IT Architect:</u>

IT architects are considered technology leaders with strong technical and non-technical skills. IT architects implement IT architecture on projects using architecture management processes, methodologies, and techniques. Refer to Chapter 2, Section 2.1 for more details.

AMBOK™ Guide:

Architecture Management Body Of Knowledge (*AMBOK™ Guide*) is a tool that has a collection of standard definitions, processes, guidelines and frameworks that are generally accepted as best practices for the IT architecture management discipline. Refer to Chapter 1, Section 1.2 for more details.

5.1.3   Benefits of Process Integration

Project managers and IT architects play a key leadership role on projects, as one provides project management leadership, and the other provides technical leadership. The strength of both roles depends on how well the roles and their management processes are understood, coordinated and integrated. Project managers need to be fully aware of how IT architects are engaged in projects and how architecture management processes are implemented. IT architects need to have a similar understanding of the project management process implementations. Project management processes have been established in the *PMBOK® Guide,* and the architecture management processes have been established in Chapter 4 of this book (*AMBOK™ Guide).*

Benefits of integrating project management and IT architecture processes include but are not limited to:

- Project managers know when and how to engage IT architects in projects.

- Project managers know the IT architect roles and accountabilities in projects.

- Project managers know how the architect deliverables need to be incorporated into project plans.

- Architects and project managers know when and how to coordinate and incorporate architecture risks, impacts, and assumptions into the project plan.

- Architects and project managers know when to work together to review and validate the estimation costs related to architecture components.

- Project managers and architects know each other's communication strategies, strengths, and responsibilities.

5.2 Process Integration Mapping

Process integration mapping highlights the important processes between project management and IT architecture. Project management processes will be referenced from the *PMBOK® Guide,* 4th edition, using process names and numbers. IT architecture processes will be referenced from Chapter 4: Architecture Management Life Cycle in this book. This section will identify project management process that IT architects are involved in and architecture processes that project managers are involved in.

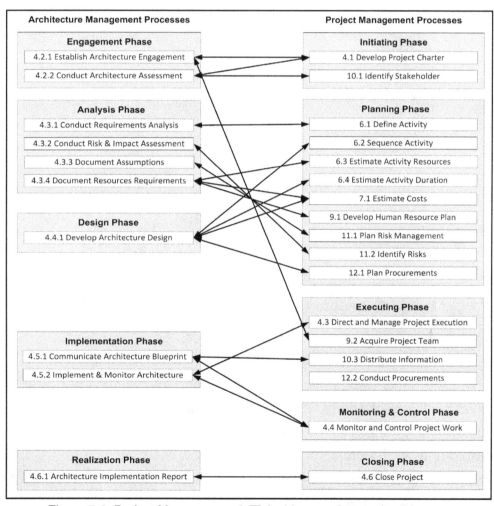

Figure 5-2. Project Management & IT Architecture Integrating Diagram

5.2.1   IT Architect Interaction in Project Management Phases

Figure 5-3 illustrates the project management's five process groupings (Initiating, Planning, Executing, Monitoring & Control and Closing) and their associated processes that require IT architect interaction.

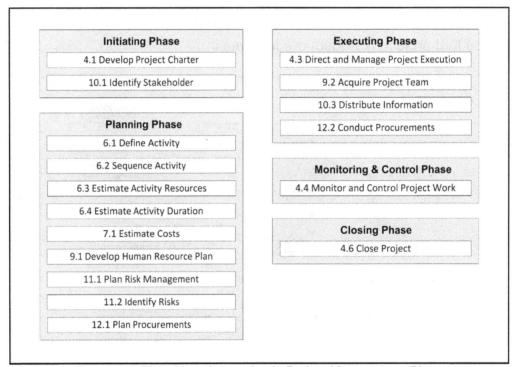

Figure 5-3. IT Architect Interaction in Project Management Phases

<u>Initiating Phase:</u>

IT architects interact with project managers during the initiating phase to review the developed project charter and indentified stakeholders. The architects can then determine if the project requires IT architecture services or not. If services are required, then the project manager will follow the architecture engagement process to request a formal architecture engagement service and update the stakeholder to include the IT architect.

PROJECT MANAGEMENT INTEGRATION

Planning Phase:

IT architects interact with project managers during the planning phase to provide input into defining, sequencing, cost estimation, resources estimation, and duration estimation related to architecture and technical domain activities. Architects can contribute in determining the technical human resource needs for the project based on the architected design and its associated components. Architects can help identify the risks, their impact, mitigation strategies and provide project managers with the required bill of material for the architecture design to include in the procurement plans.

Executing Phase:

IT architects interact with project managers during the executing phase to provide leadership in driving the technical implementation, using the approved architecture design. Architects can assist project managers in the technical team selection based on their technical expertise and frequent interaction with the technical staff. Architects work with project managers to distribute and communicate the architecture design to the technical implementation team.

Monitoring & Controlling Phase:

IT architects interact with project managers during the monitoring and controlling phase to provide technical domain knowledge, problem solving expertise, and to identify and resolve issues.

Closing Phase:

IT architects interact with project managers during the closing phase to provide input into the close project report such as lessons learned and project feedback.

5.2.2   Project Manager Interaction in IT Architecture Phases

Figure 5-4 illustrates the IT architecture's management five life cycle phases (Engagement, Analysis, Design, Implementation and Realization) and their associated processes that require project manager interaction.

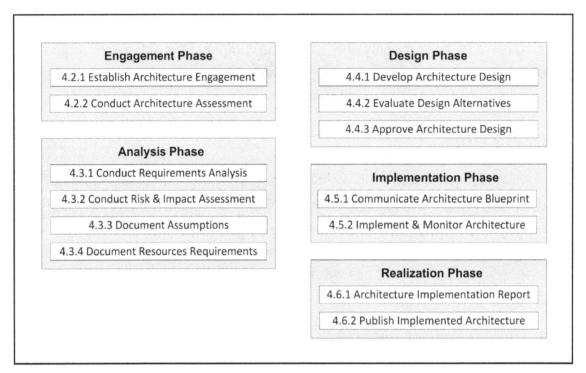

Figure 5-4. Project Manager Interaction in IT Architecture Phases

Engagement Phase:

Project managers interact with IT architects during the engagement phase to formally request an IT architecture engagement service for their project. This establishes the engagement contract, and architects can start to conduct architecture assessment to determine the scope of the work required.

Analysis Phase:

Project managers interact with IT architects during the analysis phase to help them understand the scope of the required technical and architecture components. Project managers can incorporate the architecture risks, impacts, assumptions and resources requirement into the overall project plan.

Design Phase:

Project managers interact with IT architects during the design phase to tighten up the required bill of material, cost estimates and required components based on the approved architecture design. Project managers can provide input into the evaluation criteria of the design alternative analysis, especially if project budget, timeframe and resources are impacted.

Implementation Phase:

Project managers interact with IT architects during the implementation phase to drive the overall project management activities, communication needs, and to support the IT architect technical leadership role.

Realization Phase:

Project managers interact with IT architects during the realization phase to review the architecture implementation report and to request feedback and input into the close project report.

INDEX